For Sybil, without whose absence
this book would not have come about

Doris Grumbach

Fifty Days of Solitude

BEACON PRESS · BOSTON

Beacon Press
25 Beacon Street
Boston, Massachusetts 02108-2892

Beacon Press books
are published under the auspices of
the Unitarian Universalist Association of Congregations.

Printed in the United States of America

99 98 97 96 95 8 7 6 5

Library of Congress Cataloging-in-Publication Data

Grumbach, Doris.
Fifty days of solitude / Doris Grumbach.
p. cm.
ISBN 0-8070-7060-2 (cloth)
ISBN 0-8070-7061-0 (paper)
1. Grumbach, Doris—Homes and haunts—Maine. 2. Women novelists, American—20th century—Biography. 3. Maine—Social life and customs. 4. Solitude. I. Title.
PS3557.R83Z467 1994
818′.5403—dc20
[B] 94-9373

We live, as we dream—alone.

—Joseph Conrad,
Heart of Darkness

Fifty Days of Solitude

In a letter sent to me from Hereford, England, the writer D. M. Thomas explained why he had left his academic appointment at American University in Washington, D.C., so precipitously: "It was a dreadful thing to do—my flight—but I had a sense of being in peril, as a person and as a writer (the same thing). . . . I knew that if I spent three months being 'the successful author of *The White Hotel*' I would quite likely become that and that only. I have to be the unsuccessful writer of the blank page before me."

Every ounce of acknowledgment of one's worth, however little, by the outside world, each endorsement of what I have become (no matter how insignificant), puts me in danger. In order to move forward in my work and deeper into the chambered nautilus of the mind that produces it, I need to retreat from praise from the world, from the arena of critical recognition. I must become, over and over again, Thomas's unsuccessful writer, searching desperately for ideas, furiously digging for words and images, laboring to form good sentences to fill the blank page. In any other frame of mind, if I try to write from the exhilaration of the heights instead of the despair of the depths, I am deluded about what I am doing by the falsely elevated view of what I have done.

I had been granted fifty days in the hard winter of 1993 in which to attempt a trial return to the core of myself, staying entirely alone. My companion, Sybil, had gone away to the city to search for books for her store. A strong wind had disconnected the antenna to the television set. I silenced one telephone; the other was left with instructions to the caller to leave a message but with no promise that I would return the call. I was now alone with music, books, an unpopulated cove (the ducks and gulls sensed my desire to be alone and seemed to have gone off to some other protected water farther south), and with that frighteningly reflexive pronoun, myself.

At first I found I missed another voice, not so much a voice responsive to my unexpressed thoughts as an independent one speaking its own words. On occasion, I spoke aloud, only to surprise myself. My voice sounded low, toneless, and coarse. I thought: it would be agreeable to be answered in another, more pleasing tone, even to be contradicted, gently.

There was a reward for this deprivation. The absence of other voices compelled me to listen more intently to the inner one. I became aware that the interior voice, so often before stifled or stilled entirely by what I thought others wanted to hear, or what I considered to be socially acceptable, grew gratifyingly louder, more insistent.

It was not that it spoke great truths or made important observations. No. It simply reminded me that it was present, saying what I had not heard it say in quite this way before. It began to point out the significance of the inconsequential, of what I had overlooked in my hunger for what I had always before considered to be the important, the Big Things. The noise of the world suddenly shrank to what this new voice told me, and I became aware that, with nothing to interrupt it, it now commanded my entire attention. I listened hard to it, more intently than I had to the talk of my friends in the world.

In this way, living alone in quiet, with no vocal contributions from others, no sounds (except music) from beyond my own ear, I was apt to hear news of an inner terrain, an endolithic self, resembling the condition of lichens embedded in rock.

My intention was to discover what was in there, no matter how deeply hidden, a process not unlike uncovering the treasure that accompanied the body of a Mayan king, hidden in a secret room in a tomb within a pyramid. I thought that if everything beyond myself was cut off, the outside turned inside, if I dug into the pile of protective rock and mortar I had erected around me in seventy-five years, perhaps I would be able to see if something was still living in there. Was I all *outside*? Was there enough inside that was vital, that would sustain and interest me in my self-enforced solitude? A treasure of fresh insight? A hoard (in the Wagnerian sense) of perceptions that had accumulated, unknown and unnoticed by me, in the black hole of the psyche?

I DID not cut myself off from the written words of others, figuring that there would be no interruption to an interior search if I heard only the unspoken (but unfortunately not *unheard*) voices in books. For some reason I cannot fathom I would sometimes pick up a book to read—*Moon Palace* by Paul Auster, for example—and come upon a reference to the hermetic life. In the middle of that excellent book, the painter Effing (an assumed joke-of-a-name for one of the heroes) is lost in a western canyon, finds the cave of a murdered hermit, disposes of the dead man, moves into his cave, and assumes his life.

At first he is happy:

> Then, very suddenly, this sense of calm abandoned him, and he entered a period of almost unbearable loneliness. The horror of the past months engulfed him, and for the next week or two he came dangerously close to killing himself. His mind swarmed with delusions and fears, and more than once he imagined that he was already dead, that he had died the moment he had entered the cave and was now the prisoner of some demonic afterlife. . . . After two weeks, he slowly began to return to himself, eventually subsiding into something that resembled peace of mind. It couldn't go on forever, he told himself, and that alone

> was a comfort, a thought that gave him the courage to continue.

5

There was much in that paragraph to consider, although Effing's situation differed from mine: he was hiding out from those who would surely come looking for him. But for the rest, I wondered how long I could live a completely eremitic life without losing track of reality, another way of saying that I became mad. Would limiting my social contacts to animals, as Dian Fossey did to her beloved mountain gorillas, save me from obsession and madness or perhaps, as in her case, drive me further into it?

I wondered how long it would be before the wonderful calm that commanded my mind at the start of isolation turned into unbearable loneliness. I knew what Effing learned (and Helen Yglesias reminded me of in the correspondence we carried on during my fifty days, she in Florida, I in Sargentville), that being assured of an end to the period of solitude made it possible to bear it with composure, even pleasure.

One of Effing's accomplishments in his year in the cave was to realize he had to devise a disciplined life. For two and a half months he painted, all day, every day, the magnificent landscape beyond his mountain. For the first time in his professional life he stopped worrying about results, "and as a consequence the terms 'success' and 'failure' had suddenly lost their meaning for him. The true purpose of art was not to create beautiful objects, he discovered. It was a method of understanding, a way of penetrating the world and finding one's place in it, and whatever aesthetic qualities an individual canvas might have were almost an incidental by-product of the effort to engage oneself in this struggle, to enter into the thick of things. . . . He was no longer afraid of the emptiness around him."

❧ ORDER, *sequence*, is a secret of being alone. Rising at the same time every day, making and eating breakfast while reading Morning Prayer, showering and dressing, making the bed and straightening all the rooms in which I was going to live during the day and evening. For me (but surely not for most people) this was essential: if the porch was disordered I could not start to work. This absurd obsession reminded me that one of my daughters is much like me in this respect. She needs always to have the *mudroom* in her country house clean.

Early in the morning it was cold in my study. I spent time building a fire in the woodstove, clearing my desk of bills and correspondence. Then I worked on the novel I was about half way through. The rest of the day was equally ordered: lunch, rest, work, music, reading, preparing and eating dinner, listening to the news occasionally, more reading, bed. What was inexorable about all this was the sequence of events, not to be changed or interrupted. Because if it was I was thrown back into a kind of silent, miserable chaos which nothing could dispel except to start over again at some point.

About work: Effing was right. For the first time in my writing life I gave no thought to whether I was succeeding or failing, whether what I was putting down "worked" or did not. I found I was content to examine what I was doing, in the same way that I was being taught something about the silent life. D. M. Thomas, Effing, and I were using the time to understand, to face the blank page or canvas, for instruction in ourselves, unconcerned with the judgments of others or indeed, their existence.

❧ THE *New Yorker* contained an obituary of Peter Fleischmann. It described him as "a quiet publisher," who retired when the magazine was purchased by Advance Publications (surely in this case an ironic title), and "did not talk about his separation from his beloved magazine; he simply became even quieter." Seven years later, he died. "The quietness ended in silence."

In that last sentence quietness is a mortal quality, silence the trait of death. Both existed in my isolation and solitude, so perhaps they were part of the training, as a night's fine, uninterrupted sleep is a foretaste, a trial run, for what is to come: the pleasure of death.

❧ ACCORDING to Edmond Hoyle there are twenty-three different kinds of solitaire, more than all other card games together. Sometimes solitaire is called Patience, seemingly a characteristic of playing alone and not a necessary one for games requiring more than one person.

When I was too tired to read, I played solitaire. I knew only three varieties, two of which were not described in Hoyle. I played against the bank, as I conceived my opponent to be, a solid, institutional-sounding conceit, or against the luck of the shuffle or the "tableau," the word Hoyle used for the way the cards are laid out at the start, some in rows, some in columns. Sometimes I addressed this invisible antagonist as Lady Luck. Hoyle allowed me any personification I chose to play against. He suggested Beelzebub.

I liked the idea of pitting myself against the devil (second in command after Satan in *Paradise Lost*) and decided, in line with my need for order and completeness, to try *all* the one-person games described by Hoyle. I chose them in order of my liking for their names: Accordion. Canfield. The Four Seasons. Scorpion. Fortress. A few required two packs of cards (Napoleon at St. Helena, also called Forty Thieves or Big Forty, and Spider and Tournament); they had to be ruled out because I had only one. There was something suitable about playing solitaire with a single deck of cards.

I found myself keeping a record of the games I "solved," or won or made or broke, all terms used by Hoyle. As it happened, the devil broke my game far more often than I did his. I went to bed telling him, aloud I think, that I would get back at him next time we played.

In this way, my solitude was buttressed by games named for it (the Latin *solitarius*, alone), accompanied only by invisible, powerful Satan against whom I could never successfully compete.

❧ FOR a time, sad news ripped the tapestry of my solitude. In the mail came a long obituary of my friend, the novelist and poet Kay Boyle, dead at the age of ninety. At once, the empty house seemed populated by her. Her beautiful, heavily lined face, weary, hooded eyes and omnipresent white earrings were everywhere I looked. I found her in my bedroom, seated beside me at my desk, at the kitchen table. Nothing could dispel her person. But oddly, I could not hear her voice.

Searching for it, I turned to my collection of her books and spent one evening, and then another, reading the best of her early novels, *Monday Night*, many of her fine short stories in the collection *Fifty Stories*, and two excellent novellas: *The Crazy Hunter* and *The Bridegroom's Body*. I wanted to hear her elegant, light, fictional voice, and now and again I thought I caught it in her prose.

When I saw the inscriptions she had written in these books, with her characteristic back-leaning, dark-black strokes, the kind of slant that suggests a left-handed writer, I wept. Try as I might I could not remember if she was left-handed. I could not recover her lovely, kind speaking voice, although I remembered being always aware of it when I was with her. It was as if the heavy silences in the days I was now living forbid such sound to return. It was the price I had to pay for stern exclusion of other voices; when I wished to hear a beloved one in my mind's ear I could not.

❧ WE value most what we have begun to lose: Sight. Hearing. Hair. Teeth. Mobility. Height. Friends. Old age

Kay Boyle. Photograph by Thomas Victor.

is somewhat like dieting. Every day there is less of us to be observed. It differs from dieting in that we will never gain any of it back; we must settle for what remains and anticipate further losses. I was not being philosophical about this realization, because I was not adjusted to this state of affairs. I saw it as a bald piece of information to be handed down to the confident, the worldly, the strong: in other words, the young.

❧ THREE days without a word to anyone. I have written each day to S., so I *feel* as if we have spoken, but since there were no answers (she is a poor correspondent), I am not sure. I picked up my mail at the post office and made a point to smile and nod to Carol, the new postmistress, but did not speak. I did not intend to be rude. It was that I suddenly was unsure of my voice, considering it might sound odd from misuse, or not knowing *how* it would sound.

I read my mail at home and entered future events and appointments in a new date book which contains, at the start of each month, reproductions of Edward Hopper's paintings and watercolors. Now I knew how I would illustrate my solitude. Hopper must be the only American artist with the power in his pencil and brush to portray aching loneliness on a canvas. I looked at *Early Sunday Morning* for a long time. Painted more than sixty years ago, it shows a long, two-story (Amsterdam Avenue, New York City?), red-brick building, the street-level stores dark, their canvas awnings furled, the only lit object a barber's pole in front of a shop. Upstairs, the beginning of dawn reflected in the

Edward Hopper's Early Sunday Morning *(1930). Oil on canvas, 35 × 60 inches (88.9 × 152.4 cm.). Collection of the Whitney Museum of American Art. Purchased with funds from Gertrude Vanderbilt Whitney 31.426. Copyright © 1995: Whitney Museum of American Art.*

windows, I sense the presence, in their absence, of sleepers behind the partly drawn shades and half curtains. And on the edge of the deserted yellow sidewalk stands a fire hydrant, a gray-black sturdy stumplike fixture casting a thin black shadow to parallel the longer one from the barber pole.

No one to be seen, although I know they are there, asleep, the way I know my neighbors are there, each at least two or three acres away from me and shielded from view by woods. The desertion of Hopper's street is made more bitter, intense, by the strict, straight, long line that boxes in the rectangular strip of dull, early-morning sky above the second story.

Another oil, *Two Puritans*, painted fifteen years later: Two white, old (Cape Cod?) houses side by side, one smaller than the other but with the same roofline, the same type of windows, similar doors except that the smaller one is permitted the luxury of a red cover over the door and a stern, red-brick chimney. Both have low white fences with no sign of gates. The larger house has thin, separated curtains on the front windows; otherwise all the windows, in both houses, are black to the eyes of the spectator.

But what makes this painting almost unbearably poignant are three gaunt trees that stand in the small strip of grass in front of the house and the fences. Not a branch protrudes from them; the painter has cut them off before the branching takes place, if it does. It is possible that nothing happens above that point, that they stretch on and on in their barrenness into the gray sky. They are motionless, sharp, concentrated signs of absence and desertion, within the house as well as without.

The enclosure of the houses is absolute: there are no gates to the continuous white fences. And the presence of absent (to us) persons can be sensed behind the curtains, in the black spaces that obscure the inhabitants, I surmise.

Sometimes Hopper uses figures, sad, black-outlined figures, to populate his pictures, but in one case, *Summer Evening*, he said he did not think of adding the figures of the young man and woman on the gaunt, late-night, unfurnished porch, until he had started the work. He was only interested in "the light streaming down, and the night all around."

I think he felt he could rely on empty streets, unpeopled buildings, bare tree trunks, blank windows, black tunnels, and subway exits to teach us about the terrible and beautiful isolation of nature and the human condition. Living in the world, he says, we are nonetheless alone and lonely.

Hopper is the illustrator of Virginia Woolf's dictum: "On the outskirts of every agony sits some observant fellow who points."

❧ THIS morning I realized I was not alone. The two men I was writing about in the novel called "Untitled" (in its contract) were having breakfast with me. I was asking them questions about themselves because I did not know what they were feeling, honestly feeling, at the moment I wished to take their story up again when I got back to my study. I saw their blond heads but their voices were too low for me to catch their talk; perhaps they were not talking and I was only wishing they would.

Benjamin Sachs, in Paul Auster's recent novel *Leviathan* says: "The two times I've sat down and written a novel, I've been cut off from the rest of the world, first in jail when I was a kid [he had been a conscientious objector], and now up here in Vermont, living like a hermit in the woods. I wonder what the hell it means."

Peter Aaron responds: "It means you can't live without other people. . . . When they're there for you in the flesh, the real world is sufficient. When you're alone, you have to invent imaginary characters. You need them for companionship."

So. Solitude is the proper condition for the creation of fictional characters, to keep me company, as the boys did this morning at breakfast. The longer I stayed alone, I reasoned, the greater the imaginary population of the house, the richer the fiction. If I allowed real persons to come in through the front door, they would be enough to occupy and satisfy me. I would be lost to the invented commonalty from my head.

SNOW: In mid January it arrived stealthily during the night while I slept. The first storm was merely half a foot, but it covered everything except, of course, the gray water of the cove and the protuberant rocks which were now black. It was as if a curtain had fallen on a colorful stage set and then risen on one entirely devoid of color, with only shapes to break the white monotony.

It was a most fortunate turn of events. There was no impetus to go out, no desire to uncover my car from its white corset and cap, no need for air or exercise or the sight of other persons. The snow urged me inward, to the light over my desk, to the fire in the woodstove, toward the warm, inner core of self so insulated and protected from "going out" by the snow cover that it suggested something unexpected to write about and the right way to express it.

❧ I WORKED hard the day of the first storm, feeling very pure and in tune with the climate. I thought of what Annie Fields quoted (from Aristotle) to Willa Cather in a letter: "Virtue is concerned with action; Art with production." I was not aspiring to art, but I managed to combine both virtue and production until, in the late afternoon, I was tired out. Then I filled the house with music from the last act of *Tristan and Isolde*, so loud that it obliterated the silent snow and made me feel less virtuous, less desirous of virginal ground cover and needy of some kind of warmth, some sexual reassurance. Oh well. I went up to my solitary bed, trying to hold fast to the virtues of art that flourishes in solitude and snow.

❧ THOMAS SZASZ (in *The Second Sin*): "Man cannot long survive without air, water, and sleep. Next in importance comes food. And close on its heels, solitude."

❧ THE eighteenth-century philosopher Jean-Jacques Rousseau, in *A Discourse on the Origin and Foundation of*

Inequality among Men, thought ancient man was an introvert, modern man a social being. "The savage lives within himself, while social man lives constantly outside himself and only knows how to live in the opinion of others, so that he seems to receive consciousness of his own existence merely from the judgement of others concerning him."

I wondered if both these observations were true. What evidence do we have of early human self-sufficiency? Were there hermits? Tribal life, nomadic life did not seem to allow for much solitude. Anchorites, I believe, were a Christian phenomenon, following Jesus' example of a long stay in the desert. I remembered that the trial the Maoris of New Zealand inflicted upon their young boys to prove their worthiness to enter manhood was a year alone in the wilderness, surviving all natural dangers and the more unnatural one of solitude. Such a rite of passage made a boy fit to live with the tribe. I wondered if it ever happened that it bred in him a hunger to continue to lead his life alone, in a perpetual walkabout.

But how right Rousseau was about the modern person. Our points of reference are always our neighbors, the people in the village or the city, our acquaintances at school, at games, at work, our close and distant families, all of whom tell us, with their hundreds of tongues, who we are. We are what we were told we were, we believed what we heard from others about our appearance, our behavior, our choices, our opinions. We acted according to all their instructions. Rarely if ever did we think to look within for knowledge of ourselves. Were we afraid? Perhaps, we thought, we would find nothing there. Is a person missing, an entity that can only be formed from evidence provided by someone looking at us?

We were determined by public opinions of us. Would we think we existed without outside confirmation? And how long could we live apart from others before we began to doubt our existence?

The reason that extended solitude seemed so hard to endure was not that we missed others but that we began to wonder if we ourselves were present, because for so long our existence depended upon assurances from them.

The pronouns I was using now, the generalized first person plural I used to think with in the world—we, us, our—came more easily to the pen when such matters as these suddenly concerned me. The first person pronoun makes a statement about our unique singularity of which we are only sure when we are in society. Alone, we hesitate to use it (as I am doing now) because we fear we may be talking behind the back of someone who is not there.

One thing more: Searching for the self when I was entirely alone was hazardous. What if I found not so much a great emptiness as a space full of unpleasant contents, a compound of long-hidden truths, closeted, buried, forgotten. When I went looking, I was playing a desperate game of hide-and-seek, fearful of what I might find, most afraid that I would find nothing.

❧ *THE LONG LONELINESS* by Dorothy Day. When I was alone, I was attracted to that book by its title. Dorothy

Day thought that the division between men and women could be made on the curious ground that "women especially are social beings, who are not content with just husband and family, but must have a community, a group, an exchange with others. A child is not enough. A husband and children, no matter how busy one may be kept by them, are not enough. Young and old, even in the busiest years of our lives, we women especially are victims of the long loneliness."

All this may be true for many women, for those who, in recent years, have flocked to groups offering to raise their consciousness, to workshops promising to teach them to write, to support groups for various afflictions and weaknesses. But for others, and especially for those like me who are "of a certain age," the call to come to a circle inspires only an irresistible desire to walk away, to learn what I want to know in the quiet which can never be found in a group or a community, to practice in private.

For too long women *have* existed in groups. The communities of families, of our husband's professional associates, of gatherings of other wives and mothers left together after dinner to exchange wisdom about shopping, cooking, children. The long loneliness of which Dorothy Day speaks was felt by some of us only when we were *with* other people. What we yearned for were periods of solitude to renew our worn spirits.

How seldom were most women alone, *left* alone. They went directly from a crowded childhood and young adulthood within the confines of a family to teeming dormitories at colleges and universities. Some avoided those crowds only to be given to husbands, handed over by fathers in a ceremony that emphasized the continuity of their communal existence. I lived more than half a century surrounded in this way.

I recalled two brief periods when I lived alone, the first year of World War II when my husband was drafted, and then the half-year, thirty-one years later, when we separated. With dismay I remember how I wasted those short times: I did everything I could to avoid my empty rooms; I was lonely because I had no experience with solitude. I never realized I had been given a gift; I didn't know how to use the great present of time alone. I read about it later in May Sarton's *Mrs. Stevens Hears the Mermaids Singing*: "Loneliness is the poverty of self; solitude is the richness of self."

Very late, in fact during these fifty days, I discovered the new pleasures about which Jessamyn West (in *Hide and Seek*) wrote. "Alone, alone, oh! We have been warned about solitary vices. Have solitary pleasures ever been adequately praised? Do many people know that they exist?"

DISTURBANCES to the pleasure of being alone:

The first: taxes to be paid. The old year was over. I could empty my drawer of the year's receipts and returned checks and start to figure deductions, expenses, income. A morning, then an afternoon, were lost thinking about how unprepared I was to encounter the weighty presence of the Internal Revenue Service in April. Then I was foolishly distracted from another morning's work by suddenly realizing what odd proper nouns those were. Service? How was internal revenue a service? To whom? For what? It was during such persistent, irksome worries that the small gains of solitude were lost. The world outside flooded in and drowned me in feelings of inadequacy and a hundred slips of evidential paper.

Next: misunderstandings. I had told people of my intention to be alone for a time. At once I realized they looked upon this declaration as a rejection of them and their company. I felt apologetic, even ashamed, that I would have wanted such a curious thing as solitude, and then sorry that I had made a point of announcing my desire for it. I should have hidden the fact that I wished to be alone, "like a secret vice," as Anne Morrow Lindbergh described it in *Gift from the Sea*.

To the spouse, or the long-time companion, or the family, and to the social circle, as it is called, the decision to be alone for any length of time is dangerous, threatening, a sign of rejection. "You do not like me or my company." "You are critical of me (us) and want the world to know about it." Having never felt the need to be alone themselves, having always lived happily in relationships, they looked upon my need as eccentric, even somewhat mad. But more than that, they saw it as fraudulent, an excuse to be rid of them rather than a desperate need to explore myself.

Last: page proofs of a book I had finished six months ago arrived in the middle of the fifty days. No interruption could have been more catastrophic. My isolation was flooded with errors, mistaken judgments, poor constructions, my quiet inundated with dubious opinions. In the midst of new work it was fatal to be reminded of the insufficient efforts of the past. I decided writers should be cut loose, violently, from their work when it comes out of the typewriter or the printer, the way a baby's umbilicus is severed at its birth. In this way, all errors disappear from the writer's memory, leaving the mind clear for better work, or more errors, but at least fresh ones. I had to subtract three days of solitude from the fifty I had planned in order to accommodate this intrusion.

❧ ALONE, I discovered myself looking hard at things, as if I were seeing them for the first time, or seeing them properly for the first time. I wondered if solitude promoted this activity, or whether it was a result of having more time for everything, more time to look and see, more to concentrate on what I was seeing.

I was interested in this question because so often in the past I had thought it preferable to be accompanied to the theater, to the opera, to the ballet, on travels and vacations. I had thought that there was a value to having someone along to "share" (how I have come to hate the flat, soft, sentimental sound of that word) the experience. But I began to see in these weeks alone that a greater value lay in hearing and seeing from within that mysterious inner place, where the eyes and ears of the mind are insulated from the need to communicate to someone else what I experienced. The energy necessary to express myself to someone else seemed to have been conserved for the harder look, the keener hearing.

❧ BY chance, as I was considering this, I came upon Susanne K. Langer's *Problems of Art*. She quotes the art critic Roger Fry's view that, because of the needs of everyday existence, "the sense of vision becomes highly specialized in their service. We learn to see only what serves our immediate purposes, what we need to see. Useful objects 'put on more or less the cap of invisibility,' and are seen only so far as practicality allows."

But, he says, "it is only when an object exists in our lives for no other purpose than to be seen that we really look at it." This, in his terms, is "pure vision abstracted from necessity."

Langer thinks that the only way to separate pure vision from the fabric of real life is to create it, so that what I was looking at was "nothing but appearance," the unreal becomes real because I have written it (or composed or painted it).

Just recently I learned the truth of this. The real occupants of the house were the two young men I had put into my fiction, more actual than I was, the "real" tenants of my study and kitchen. I believed they were here and so I saw them far more clearly than the pictures of my grandchildren or drawings framed on the walls.

Fry and Langer were not concerned with the fate of ordinary objects when, in quiet and isolation, I looked hard at them. But I found that interesting. They turned into *new* objects, seen in a curious, hard original light, no longer ordinary or familiar.

ঌ ROBERT A. ROSENSTONE, *Mirror in the Stone*:

> A Japanese artist was commissioned by an American to do a painting. The completed work had, in a lower corner, the branch of a cherry tree with a few blossoms and a bird perched upon it. The entire upper half of the painting was white. Unhappily, the American asked the artist to put something else in the painting because it looked, well, so bare. The Japanese refused the request. When pressed for an explanation, the artist said if he did fill up the painting, there would be no space for the bird to fly.

Many years ago I bought a colored etching from Donald Furst, an artist then living in Iowa. Called *Into White*, it is filled in the top seventh of the rectangular page with winter trees and distant snow-covered fields. The rest of the long sheet is white, untouched by any lines or colors, so that most of the work is blank, leaving a great deal of space for the snow to lie heavy and impenetrable on the ground. I went to my wall to look hard at *Into White*, at the pure snow of my imagination, the way the Japanese artist must have seen, clearly, the bird in flight.

Another lesson learned in solitude: To look hard at what I did not notice before and even harder at what is not there, at what Paul Valéry called "the presence of absence."

❧ MY solitude was, for a long time, untroubled because I had ruled out all news and thoughts of racial disturbance in cities and on campuses, ethnic cleansing in Bosnia, social upheaval, civil wars, revolution, starvation, and homelessness everywhere. If I failed to read the newspaper or listen to the radio, they seemed not to exist.

Nothing outside the house, beyond the woods and the cove, was happening. But that tranquil state did not last. In the third week I was informed, by letter, that Tracy Sampson's brother Craig, who came to dinner at our house last fall, had died of AIDS in San Francisco. At the same time, in the mail, came word from Ed Kessler, my former colleague in the English department at American University, that his friend Jim, whom we had known well in Washington, had been murdered in Boston, presumably by some toughs he had befriended when he was ill. And a week later I learned that my small granddaughter Hannah was slated to have her skull cut open by a plastic surgeon to correct a slight birth defect on her forehead and one eye.

Through the most minute crack, the catastrophes and tragedies of the world outside intruded upon the serenity of my life. A death by cruel virus, a murder by knife, an operation-to-come on a one-year-old relative have left their unmistakable mark, like the piste of a wild animal.

❧ LOOKING hard at what I had not noticed before—the shape of snow around the bird feeder where the feet of birds have tramped a wide circle in their search for fallen bird seed, the lovely V-shaped wake of a family of newly arrived eider ducks as they cross the cove, the sight of a green log sputtering and drooling sap in the woodstove as if in protest against my feeding it prematurely to the flames—was tiring. The weight of new experience, the storing of it on the front burner of my memory, and then recovering it for use in this record: all this took more energy than the old, careless, eyes-once-over-the-object practice.

In these days alone, was I perhaps preparing myself for the final deep freeze, the eternal hibernation, the last, empty room, the eventual, never-to-be interrupted solitude: death? and the deaf-and-dumb, blind, under-restraints quietus: dying?

❧ SNOW again. Trees were reduced to white skeletons. Still there was a towering greatness to them, stretched to their great white heights. The little new crabapple tree was now a mere sketch. Familiar shapes were transformed into indecipherable humps, mounds, gravelike knolls, the "alabaster chambers," as Emily Dickinson called them. It was hard to remember that under the blankness lived seeds, bulbs, and roots, perennial and phoenixlike, immortal in a way. It was only the deceptive appearance of death I was staring out at, which, after all, is not death at all.

❧ WOULD I have been as content alone if it were not for the beauty of this place? Was it true, as Sybil asserted time and again, that I cared more for the cove than for company? Would a prisoner be happier tied into a hut alone but within sight of the sea than if he were jailed in a windowless cell?

I was reading E. M. Forster's *Howard's End* one evening when I came upon this interchange. Margaret says: "It is sad to suppose that places may even be more important than people."

Helen asks: "Why, Meg? They're so much nicer generally. . . ."

Margaret: "I believe we shall come to care about people less and less, Helen. The more people one knows, the easier it becomes to replace them."

❧ ONE early morning I came downstairs to make coffee. I sat before the kitchen window looking out to the black sea to watch the sunrise. Tired of waiting for it, I began to read, became engrossed, looked up after a while to find that streaks of brilliant yellow light had filled the sky over the reach. I was disappointed at having missed the moment when the spectacle arrived, the way one must feel if one has watched at a death bedside for a long time, gone out for a breath of air, and come back to find the beloved dead.

The sky grew more startling—red, blue clouds, the horizon at Deer Isle almost black—and I watched for a while. But, despite the wonder of the sight, my interest waned again. I went back to the book I had been reading, Elizabeth Drew's *The Modern Novel*, in which she says that "the test of literature is, I suppose, whether we ourselves live more intensely for the reading of it."

No, I thought. At the moment I missed the sunrise by looking too closely at the printed page, I had diminished my life in a curious way. The intensity literature aroused in me, I believe, was often less than what happened when I listened to, felt, and saw the world around me.

❧ I FOUND there was a relation between cold and silence. The temperature in my bedroom at night was usually less than fifty degrees. The silence, the absence of another person, intensified the cold. The cold made the silence absolute. It seemed to lower the temperature of the room and to extend the size of it. Death is the great cold, I thought, and turned on the radio. Sound, I found, was somewhat warming, even the sound of a talkative host interrogating sleepless callers who wanted to air their views about the state of the world's evils.

I was dressed for the cold, having put on a flannel nightgown and bathrobe, a woolen scarf, high woolen socks, a Navy watch cap, and a pair of Sybil's old mittens. They rendered my hands useless for turning the pages of Marian Engel's novel *The Bear*, which I had taken upstairs to reread before I went to sleep. Sybil's mother had brought the furred sacks back from the Soviet Union years ago, and now they were stretched, overly large, but wonderfully warm and comforting. They conjured up Sybil's presence. I put Engel on the floor, turned out the light, moved further down under the quilt, and, in the absence of sound and cold, in the imagined company of an absent friend, fell asleep.

❧ I DECIDED I would break my quietus by going to church on Sundays and on Wednesdays, for midday liturgy. I resolved to arrive late, just as the services were starting, and to leave at the moment the final words of blessing were spoken, in order to avoid the pleasant chitchat that always surrounded ecclesiastical rites at St. Francis. I managed to do this, leaving behind, I imagined, startled parishioners who remarked to each other about my sudden unsociability and wondered if I had gone "all queer," as they say up here.

Did I think talking to my acquaintances would affect the purity of my fifty days? I suppose I did, being an intolerant absolutist and believing, I think, that any break in the tapestry of silence would cause the whole plan, the unconditional experiment, to come undone.

In the afternoon I worked for a while, keeping the fire going in the woodstove in the living room. Then I lay down under the afghan my daughter Elizabeth Cale had crocheted for me and finished *The Bear*. It is about a lonely woman, working in the isolation of an island in Northern Canada, who finds companionship and then love, yes, with a bear. I read the novel nearly twenty years ago for the *New York Times Book Review* and was impressed and startled by its originality. I had never heard of the Canadian writer Marian Engel, so I went to the Library of Congress and read her six previous novels, all in order to report that *The Bear* was unique among her writings.

The other night I found the book again and reread it, to see how Lou, the librarian-researcher of early settlements in Canada, dealt with her time alone on Cary Island, alone except for the bear that had been chained up by the previous owner of the place behind the curious octagonal house Lou inhabited. At first she discovered she was listening to tiny sounds of small bird-feet in dry leaves, the river sucking at reeds and stones, the cracking of branches.

But then she found herself "hating to disturb the precious felted silence" inside the house. "She filled the kettle, nervously scraping the dipper against the pail. She dressed and heard the tearing noises of her clothes. She stomped her shoes on and heard the laces whirring against each other as she tied them. She scraped the butter knife against her toast. Stirred her coffee with a jangling spoon. Not everyone, she thought, is fit to live with silence."

I had noticed the singular and disturbing effect of a little sound in a quiet house, especially a noise I did not anticipate. Sitting at the computer I jumped when I had to adjust the Velcro-fastened straps of my wrist band. Velcro is noisy, much louder than a zipper, totally unlike a button or hook and eye which make no sound at all. Closure with them, to use Engel's good word, is felted. But Velcro: The arrangement of dense nylon hooks on one tape tears at the other one of nylon pile making a ripping noise that grated on my ear. It was not that I was not fit to live with silence, but rather that I was unprepared for its interruption.

Perhaps the time would come when I could no longer bear it, after I had made an effort to spend hours without activating disturbances: doing a wash, rinsing the dishes, walking on the bare floor in heavy shoes. There was so much silence in my days that I had become aware of it only when a sound stopped: the refrigerator going off, the toilet ceasing to flush, the rain no longer falling on the steps. But I considered the possibility that quiet might become as oppressive as noise, that silence, unlike the harsh, unacceptable sounds that bounce off my ears like stones, could bring tears to my eyes and break my heart.

❧ BOOKS arrived, unbidden, in their hard brown mailers, unexpected titles I would never think to read if they were not delivered to my door, hopeful gifts from publishers who think I might recommend them to others. One day Maria Riva's biography of her mother, Marlene Dietrich, came, a thick book (almost eight hundred pages) that vacillated between general admiration of the actress's accomplishments, strong will, and creative skill at transforming herself into myth and legend and then particular dialogue that destroyed every bit of the celluloid vision we had all grown to revere.

It took two full days of my hoarded time to read the book. I was fascinated by it all, despite the doubts about its veracity that crept in after the first hundred pages. Until then the evidence about Dietrich's early career came from letters she wrote to her husband, entries she kept in her diary, and copies of letters from her lovers she sent on to her ever-patient husband.

But on page 101 there are three long paragraphs, occupying the whole page, of direct quotation from Dietrich in conversation with her husband, overheard and then reported by her daughter who, at the time, was six years old. We are told that the actress, as she spoke, was eating stuffed cabbage, before that she had munched "on a hunk of pumpernickel, loaded with goose fat." A paragraph later "she took another dill pickle."

What was I to think? What could I believe? That the child Maria retained and then produced, without question or paraphrase, these hundred or so sentences verbatim? That, in addition, she could recall the exact food her mother ate on that day more than fifty years ago? Of course, it could be said that she remembered the *kind* of nourishment her mother had preferred in her younger years, but these exact details, first the cabbage, then the pickles? It boggled my mind.

From this point on, unless I was given a letter or a diary entry, I questioned everything I read. This was too bad, because Maria knew her mother well enough to claim she might well have said these outrageous things about everyone she met or knew: her sharply critical custom was to talk in this manner all her life apparently. It was, I decided, the ubiquitous presence of all those quotation marks that made me doubt her narrative. Until the last fifty pages, that is, when she told the story of her ninety-year-old mother's tragic end as a recluse, unable to walk, stranded in a soiled and reeking bed (which she refused to allow anyone to clean), drunk most of the time, drugged the rest.

Holding on desperately to a life she was too frightened to give up, and to a vision she had of herself provided by an adoring public that she could not bear to see updated, Dietrich lived on, sick, closeted, deluded, and furious that the fate of her aged body was common to all who lived long, resentful that she was not uniquely and youthfully preserved as she thought she deserved to be. I found it easy to believe every word of this, not only because the direct dialogue here could perhaps have been remembered (more or less) by her daughter who came often to Paris to see her, but because Maria Riva's description of her mother's final state rang so true to my vision of the end beautiful women often came to when the surface they have spent their lives relying upon was lost.

For Dietrich, the hardest loss, worse than friends, lovers, admirers, hearing, health, and agility, was the youthful state of her face and her legs. It seemed to me tragic to have the sense of one's self dependent on these transient things, so that old age is spent in a constant state of mourning for lost beauty. It is the fate of those who had it to begin with, nurtured it, relied on it, used it, and discovered at the last that it was the *sine qua non* of their lives. There was little else.

CARE in the use of language came with seldom hearing it or using it aloud. I discovered that when I began to write in those dark, early mornings I approached the whole act of word choice warily. I attributed this to not wasting my verbal energies in hearing talk and in speaking. Every word I put down on paper seemed to take on a kind of holiness, a special, single precision (to use a computer term in a different sense), resembling not at all the usual detritus that was left over after spurts of talk.

I realized that inconsequential conversation, and television and radio talk, had deafened me to careful usage and to precision in syntax, in sentence structure, in word choice. Now when I spoke aloud, as I did occasionally to fill an oppressive space of silence, I uttered some spontaneous foolishness. When I ended a long, soundless spell by taking up my clipboard to write, I proceeded slowly, carefully, feeling I had to consider *each letter* of every word, because quiet and unlimited time produced a boundless prospect for choice.

❧ I WAS not the only living creature in the house. A horde of large black flies had taken refuge around the window frames in the bedrooms. Prudently, they had come in from the cold to live as long as they could in a milder climate. I wondered what sustenance they found on the wood and glass of the southeast windows, but I understood their affinity for the radiating sun. As long as they did not come closer in search of greater warmth when I was reading in bed I practiced my usual tolerance for living things and my dislike of killing them under any pretext.

But one night my lamp, my book, and I were attacked by an extended family of flying seekers after light and heat. My first instinct was to slap at them madly. So inept was I (I was wearing Sybil's Soviet mittens) that I missed them all and succeeded only in sending them back to their old berths in the window. I turned out the light so they would not be tempted to return, although I was not tired and wanted to continue reading. But I felt the truce that we had formed in the darkness—they in their place, I in mine—was preferable to mass slaughter. Eventually, pleased with my pacifism, I fell asleep.

❧ ONE morning there were huge black crows at the feeder, and no one else. They seemed to have frightened the small birds away permanently. Forty or so eider ducks remained in the cove, swimming decorously, almost parading, across the frigid water in the morning and back again at dusk. I shuddered to think how cold they must be and then applauded their gallantry at not leaving me for the Caribbean or the Gulf of Mexico.

Befriended in this way—by crows and ducks and black flies—how could I feel lonely or alone in this place?

❧ DID I think more about age, aging, being and growing old when I was alone? I think so. I had no resident check on my despair, no one to point out how lucky I was to *be* here in order to despair. Solitude became the rich breeding ground for my natural depression because I had ruled away every possible deterrent: phone calls, dinners out, television, even the radio most of the time, preferring to choose the music I wished to hear on tapes or CDs.

I played operatic music and musicals while I worked, and one day reduced myself to tears by listening to *La Cage aux Folles*. In its uncritical, sentimental way, it celebrates elderly love, fidelity, and acceptance between lovers of the same sex. I could not bear it and had to change the tape to something chillier, more coldly classic: Bach, I think it was.

When I am among people I have usually been able to forget, or bury, or disguise, my despondency. Without company I have had to remember that despair is always lurking beyond the circle of lamplight, the flames of the woodstove, the warmth of the gas oven. If I took steps into any dark place I was once again afraid, despairing, and aware of how old I was and how young I would give anything to be.

SOMEONE once told me that my mind was too Gothic, that my mental life was lived in dark, medieval towers and dungeons. What I needed, he said, was brighter, more cheerful interior decoration. I thought about this, in one of those evenings when I was "low," and decided that when I was young my Buckminster Fuller mind was furnished with Marcel Breuer furniture and Formica countertops, but there occurred a rapid retreat as I grew older, a relapse into the decor of Edward and Victoria.

IN search of parallels to my experience, to what it was like to walk out on the bare deck and see the moonlit night sky and the frozen waters of the reach, I remembered that Beryl Markham, the intrepid pilot of a small plane that delivered mail in east Africa in the 1930s, wrote in her autobiography (*West with the Night*) about sitting by a campfire before the tents with a few natives and two friends, Bror Blixen and Winston Guest, meditating on primordial Africa:

> It was a world as old as Time, but as new as Creation's hour had left it. . . . In a sense it was formless. When the low stars shone over it and the moon clothed it in silver fog, it was the way the firmament must have been when the waters had gone and the night of the Fifth Day had fallen on creatures still bewildered by the wonder of their being. It was an empty world because no man had yet joined sticks to make a house or scratched the earth to make a road or embedded the transient symbols of his artifice in the clean horizon. But it was not a sterile world. It held the genesis of life and lay deep and anticipant under the sky.
>
> You were alone when you sat and talked with the others—and they were alone. . . . What you say has no ready ear but your own, and what you think is nothing except to yourself. . . . You talk, but who listens? You listen, but who talks?

A distant lion "stalks in a distant silence. A jackal skirts the red pool of comfort that warms you," the native boy warns that the lion is hungry tonight. "But Simba is not hungry. He is alone, too, companionless in his courage, friendless in his magnificence—uneasy in the night. He roars, and so he joins our company, and hyenas join it, laughing in the hills. And a leopard joins it, letting us feel his presence, but hear nothing. Rhino—buffalo—where are they? Well, they are here too—somewhere here—just there, perhaps, where that bush thickens or that copse of thorn trees hides the sky. They are here, all are here, unseen and scattered, but sharing with us a single loneliness. . . .

"Somebody attempts to break the loneliness. It is Blix, asking a simple question that everybody answers, but nobody has listened to."

Why did I read these pages again and again? Because the sense of absolute aloneness is there, despite the presence of other persons and hovering wild animals. Beryl Markham knew that one could be alone surrounded by all this, perhaps even more alone because of it, not listening so one did not hear, feeling presences without seeing them, so concentrated in oneself and one's own thoughts that no one, nothing else existed. At the end she called this loneliness: They were all, human beings and animals, partaking of a single loneliness, the universal solitude in which we all have lived, try as we might to escape it in company, in entertainment, in family gatherings, while making love.

I DID not find solitude easier to live in or accept the longer I stayed alone. No, every day I found I had to work harder to maintain it. From the exhilaration and self-satisfaction of the first days, when I went into training for it, turning meetings and inquiries and visitors and machinery and appliances off, living productively in it was never easy.

Sudden strokes of neediness struck me. One night I tired of the thought of making dinner and longed to go out for someone else's cooking. Increasingly, I wearied of the exercise of listening hard to hear and of staring at objects to see them more clearly and more enduringly. The words I put on paper, at first so prinked out in elaborate language, staled. Ideas that arose out of the well of loneliness after a while seemed moribund if not actually dead. And then, what was I to do? I emulated Mark Twain's person sitting alone in darkness and bemoaned my failures.

I noticed that my mail, in this period, contained an inordinate amount of bad news. Friends wrote to let me know about deaths and, in one sad case, the imminent trial of a priest-friend on seven felony counts of grand larceny.

Letters that contained obituaries from newspapers were kindly meant, I knew. The writers assumed (rightly in both cases) that "up there" I would not have heard or read the news. But always, the day bad news arrived became a useless one. I felt like an epiphyte, that tropical plant that takes its nourishment not from the soil or sand but from the air. Every breath of air I took seemed full of doom.

I needed to take a walk to the road and back after I learned of the death of Dr. Perkins. I had to get out of the stale, dire house air. Anna Perkins was doctor to Sybil's family and to most people in the rural hill towns of East Berne, Westerlo, and Clarksville in upstate New York. For sixty-five years, after her graduation from Radcliffe College and Columbia University Physicians and Surgeons Medical School, she made the rounds of her largely poor patients, farmers and working men and women, treating and dosing them for her fee of $5 a visit. Sometimes she forgot to collect the fee and had to be reminded or accepted a chicken or eggs in its place. Sybil told me that once, having treated her son Chris at home for a high fever,

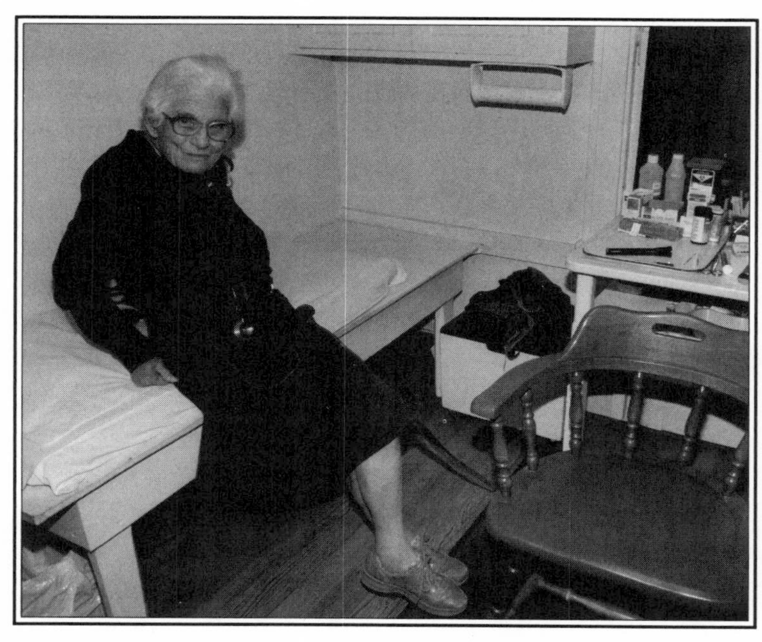

Dr. Anna Perkins. Photograph courtesy of the Times-Union, *Albany, New York.*

Dr. Perkins flatly refused to accept any money. "I was passing your house anyway," she said.

One day I went on her rounds with her. She was then in her mid-seventies, I believe. She would pull up to a farmhouse and begin to gather her equipment as the farmer's wife (or husband or daughter) came down the path, helped her out of her Land Rover, and carried her bag to the house. I waited in the car, studying the list of places she intended to visit, the names of the chronically ill or the sick who had called, their complaint, and what medicine she intended to administer. The back of her car was crowded with free samples from drug companies, her own vials of medicines she dispensed to families who could not afford them, and her well-worn missal; her day always started at the Catholic church with early mass.

Visits to her office, from the day she began to practice medicine in 1928 until she died in 1993, cost $4. She was not the prototypical country doctor who sticks stubbornly to what she once learned. Every Thursday she drove to the medical center in Albany to attend the weekly seminars on recent advances in medical knowledge and practice. She read the current literature (I know this from the journals I saw in her van) together with the customary Catholic fare: *America*, *Catholic Mind*, the papal encyclicals.

She had not always been alone. Her companion of forty years was the daughter of a local industrial family, whom she always referred to as Miss Hannay. Miss Hannay died in 1973. Ten years later, when Sybil and I visited Dr. Perkins, she was still grieving for her. "It does not get any easier," she told us, and then said nothing more.

She did not go to Harvard Medical School, she told us, because in her time it would not accept women. . . . She treated five generations of the Hannay family. . . . During storms she used to put on snowshoes to reach stranded families with sick children and once was air-lifted by helicopter to care for a patient with a bad heart who lived in the hills. . . . Out on her rounds if she saw a child playing in the yard who was supposed to be in bed, she would stop her car, order him indoors, and chastise the child's parent. . . . Sybil once complained to her that her hands and feet were always cold. She wondered if she might be anemic. "Try turning up the thermostat," was her advice. . . . She was an avid lover of animals and, spotting a deer in a field during hunting season, would blow her horn loudly to scare it back into the wood. . . . Once she took her chair and sat in front of a tree she wished to save from the axes of road builders.

I did not know her well. Few people did: She was a very private woman who did not air her aches or griefs and disappointments. Sybil knew her better, and loved her, and thought of her every time she paid her Washington internist three hundred dollars for a physical examination.

ONE of the elderly nuns at the College of Saint Rose, where I taught for almost ten years in the 1960s, wrote to me of the death of my longtime friend Sister Noel Marie Cronin, at eighty-three, in retirement at her order's motherhouse, as it is called, and having served her vows faithfully for more than sixty years. She suffered from osteoporosis. She too was a woman of unusual reticence, who never to my knowledge talked about herself—I cannot recall her ever using the first person pronoun. She taught mathematics at the college. In her free time, deeply concerned for the future of young blacks in the South End ghetto of Albany, she organized a summer tutorial program at the college called GAP (Growth and Progress). She taught high school students math, persuaded other college personnel to teach English, dramatics, history, and science, and saw to it that the college provided lunch, snacks, and classroom space for "her kids." She was unforgiving of carelessness, thoughtless behavior, and bad manners; but the kids respected her, some even loved her, and certainly they obeyed her.

Noel (I would not have dared to address her in this way anywhere but in print, and after her death, but I thought of her as Noel) never asked me for money to support GAP once I had left the college. Instead she would write to me regularly in Washington, D.C., reporting on the progress and growth of one or another of her prize pupils and telling me some news of the faculty.

She was the daughter of deeply religious parents. Three of her brothers became priests and another sister and brother never married. I often speculated on whether strong puritanical teachings about sex had discouraged these children. All I knew for certain about Noel's sentiments was that when she heard an alumna had married she would wrinkle up her nose in distaste and say nothing.

I never heard her utter a critical word about a priest. Her

devotion to the clergy was absolute. She was fond of Father Sam Wheeler who later left the priesthood to marry my daughter. She wrinkled her nose when she heard the news, but she said nothing disparaging to me about him and certainly never seemed to hold his disaffection against me.

When I heard of her death I pictured her as I first saw her, a small, bent woman in her old floor-length black habit, looking up into the face of a six-foot black lad, he with his hands on his hips looking down at her and protesting something. I saw her shake her head and point, and then the boy sat down at an outdoor picnic bench on the campus and took up a pencil and paper. She stood looking over his shoulder watching him work out some algebraic equations.

I walked away after that, but the tableau has remained with me. Wherever she is now she is doubtless laying down the laws of trigonometrical functions to a boy about to take the entrance exam to some celestial sphere or other.

❧ THE news that disturbed me most, that unsettled me to the point of a wasted morning's work, because all semblance of peace had departed from my study, concerned one of Sister Noel's favorite priests, Father Bertrand Fay. Tall, handsome, and very charming, he was my friend too. We spent many happy hours together listening to his superb recordings of opera in his quarters at the college, the same house in which Sam Wheeler lived before he defected into marriage with my daughter.

Years ago, when Bert was the object of unproven accusations of sexual "deviation" against him and Father Richard Lucas, both of them teachers in the department of theology, Noel was one of Bert's firmest defenders. (I have always thought that to her innocent mind a priest could not possibly be guilty of any sort of wrongdoing.) The unpleasant brouhaha ended in the resignation of the college president, who had issued the terminal contracts to him and to Richard, and the departure of Richard from the college, the church, and the city because (this is my guess) he could no longer bear to be dishonest, to play the closeted role he had been forced into.

For many years after that Bert and I exchanged Christmas presents. He would send me a magnificent poinsettia plant; I would, on occasion, give him whatever new book on opera I could find. Poinsettia was a flower Sybil disliked, but we could not figure out a way to cut off the thoughtful and (to my way of thinking) very handsome gift.

Bert was well-to-do, having a good salary and being the only child of wealthy parents. One after the other they died, leaving money to their beloved son. He moved out of the college into an apartment. With a close friend he set up an antiques business, after that a good restaurant. Both seem to have failed. For many years, a much-admired priest who was considered a fine preacher, he went on teaching at the college and serving a nearby parish on Sunday.

He must have run out of money. He must have needed it

to go on living the good life he found important ("He dressed very well," one parishioner told a reporter, a bad

thing, I suppose he thought, for a priest to do). Someone else told me Bert felt he deserved the good life.

Apparently Bert still went to New York during the opera season. Did he keep the same subscription tickets he had had for so many years? I have no way of knowing. It was said he had two apartments in New York, but I don't know if this was true.

All I knew for certain was what I read in the long clippings sent to me from the *Albany Times-Union* and the *Troy Record*. It would appear that recently he had begun to borrow money from priest-friends, former nuns, senior citizens, and friends, on the pretext that it was an investment (to be repaid at 18 percent interest) in important work being done at the college by a student who was expecting large grants for his research in entomology. When very little of the more than a quarter million dollars in loans was repaid, Bert said the student had died of AIDS and his family was withholding the money.

There was, of course, no department of entomology at the college, nor any student registered there who was doing research in the field. Bert gave up his college post, which he had held for twenty-five years, and left the priesthood. He now faced foreclosure on a house he allegedly collateralized with the money he borrowed, as well as numerous counts of grand larceny. He was out on bail.

I felt great pity for Bert even while I recognized the wrongs he may have done to trusting persons and the selfishness of satisfying his own needs at great cost to others. If he is convicted, his will be a tragic fall, from the heights of respect and admiration granted a priest and professor, especially if he is handsome, graceful, and charming, from prosperity and every kind of pleasure, to the lower depths of a probable jail sentence and the life-long distrust, even scorn, of his acquaintances and friends. How will he live with this descent during the years he has before him?

American society leads to many more precipitous falls than ascents that move steadily upward through a lifetime. It is one of the tragedies of a very promising youth that too often achievement and recognition come early and too fast, leaving a long life of disappointment and decline. At the same time, those who start slowly are more fortunate. With few expressed hopes for their futures and only their own convictions, they quietly and in obscurity make their way up whatever ladder they wish to ascend. Success in middle and old age is gratifying, especially since it makes more bearable all the physical failures of those years.

IN WHAT odd places we must go to find solitude! A physician I know told me that he did not mind one whit having an examination known as Magnetic Resonance Imaging (MRI), a diagnostic procedure most people hate because the patient is encased for so long, lying still in a machine that is almost tomblike. He said it was the only quiet time he had had in a long time, and he was able to think very well in the stillness and silence the examination provided.

❧ ONE day last week the newspaper contained a review of a new book, *The First Year: A Retirement Journal* by John Mosedale. It startled me because so much of Mosedale's initial concern about retirement ran counter to mine. Without the presence of the storm and strife of the work-a-day world, he said he feared that untroubled retirement would not be a continuous pleasure. He told a story of a man who lived on a South Pacific island: "Life was effortless. Each day the sun rose in splendor. One morning the man emerged from his hut, looked at the rising sun and said, 'Another perfect goddamned day' and shot himself."

Mosedale worried about "the sudden silence after the roar of work." I remember that when I moved to Maine (retirement in the strict sense is not required of writers) I could not wait for the moment when quiet would descend upon me, only to discover that silence was not a state often granted to anyone, however one might desire it. In the fifty days in which I worked to achieve it, I learned how elusive it was. The far-off sound of a passing car, the whine of a chain saw in the distance—at my neighbor's house a quarter of a mile away, was it?—the rough quack of crows searching for sustenance in the snow under the bird feeder, the crack and snap of a log falling into the woodstove ashes, these were the breaks in my silence. They roughed up the smooth nothingness I hoped for.

Mosedale said he thinks much less about death now that he is approaching it than he did as a young man. "I don't avoid the thought. I am just not interested." Curious. When I was alone in my relative silence I thought about it a great deal. I realized that at my age it had become part of the very texture of my thinking. Everything was related to its imminence: my reading, the music I heard, my sense of time and place, my plans, my prayers, my very appetite for thought, for work, for sleep. Perhaps in this sense I not so much *thought* about death as lived with it, like a mortal illness or the loss of a leg. It was not indifference, quite the contrary. It was interest so profound I could not for a moment escape its occupation of my life.

I SPOTTED an eagle very high in the sky over the cove, making its easy way through a blank sky. It made me think of a Franciscan nun I read about in the local newspaper who died of cancer after a lifetime of devotion to the poor, the homeless, the hungry in Hancock County where I live. Shortly before her death, her caretaker told her an eagle was flying over her house. "Tell it to wait," Sister Barbara said. "That's my ride."

"I CAN'T hear myself think." I must have said that many times in my lifetime. The cliché may have been preceded by: "The noise they (the children, the neighbors) make in the house (or apartment) next door is so great that, etc." When I set the conditions for thought, in those blessed days and nights, I discovered it was sometimes very hard to hear what I was thinking, not because of any exterior noise, but, strangely enough, because of the overpowering silence. I had to listen hard (as I had learned the importance of looking hard) to hear what I was thinking, or even to discover whether I was thinking at all. I needed my ears to catch the gossamers of thought that I would have believed more substantial and more independent of those organs.

I have always known that without words placed in logical relation to each other I had no thoughts, am not, indeed, thinking, contrary to what students used to say to me: "I know what I mean but I can't say it." It turned out that the words in which my thinking was necessarily couched were hard to catch, because the tone, the voice, was mine, and I had grown immune to that voice. Try as I might to listen, I found I had become bored with the *sound* of my own thoughts embedded in that old, omnipresent voice, and so I stopped listening. This, I discovered, was one of the unavoidable disadvantages of being alone.

In the silence I eagerly sought, I *could* hear myself think, and what I heard was, sadly, often not worth listening to.

ONE long, very dark night, I found myself fantasizing about the vague sounds I heard in the attic above my head. I told myself the reason so few old homes harbor the ghosts of those who have lived and died there is because those unsubstantial figures are dispelled, frightened off, by the multitudinous in-house noises of today: the furnace, the refrigerator, washing and drying machines, the dishwasher and Disposall, electric clocks, all of these things, and more.

Quiet houses are hospitable to ghosts. They flourish

there. I know this because, one night when the power failed, so that all the appliances were silenced, no car moved along the road, and I lay upstairs in bed without the intrusive, tinny sound of the battery-radio, I thought I heard Ella Byard, who built this house before she married Captain Willis White, moving about in the hall downstairs.

Then my fantasy grew. I thought I heard her walking to the porch to sit in the sunlight of a cool August afternoon with her women friends and relatives, exactly as the ten of them appear on the back of a postcard given to me by Connie Darrach, one of her descendants in Sargentville. I saw that it was the porch of another house down the road from me, and I remembered Mrs. Darrach telling me the women gathered together every year to celebrate the birthday of her grandmother. Ella Byard is front left, birdlike and elegant. Addie France, smiling and apparently toothless and wrapped in a shawl, is behind her. Aunt Mae Millikan is bespectacled and very pleasant looking. Emma Gray is next to Faustina Dodge who is wearing a fine black hat and is looking away from the camera. Ella is near her relative Abby Byard, white-haired, handsome, and all in black satin, and Lydia Byard Sargent Gower whose ruffled collar frames a thin neck and a thoughtful, almost grim face. Sweet-faced Dora Currier is all in white, rather ghostly among the black-satined other ladies like solemn Lucia Means who sits between her and gloomy, straw-hatted, bespectacled Serena Turner. The occasion appears to be in the 1920s.

Ella Byard and friends. Photograph courtesy of Connie Darrach.

Their sloping shoulders, their drawn-back white hair, their hands folded comfortably in their laps, the ten old ladies respond to the camera's action as if they knew this was a signal moment in their elderly histories, that life might not catch them all together in this way again. In my fantasy they are thus unexpectedly reunited, but this time on my porch, populating my quiet, almost empty house with their ancient shadows, satisfying my sudden need for people.

❧ KENNY GRINDLE once owned our house, perhaps twenty years ago. Now he lives in a tiny shack down and across the road from us. He has few amenities, no telephone, no television, no car. He relies on neighbors for his occasional forays to the general store and on his radio for the news. He heats with a wood stove so his strip of yard on the state road is strewn with logs which he splits himself and with odd bottles and miscellaneous objects he offers to passersby in a perpetual yard sale. Now and again, in a fit of assertive desire for isolation, he tacks up on his trees four cardboard signs that warn motorists to KEEP OUT.

He is elderly, suffering from emphysema and the remnants of a hard life, yet his opinions about what is important in life remain firm. Sometimes he and his clothes smell musty. I wonder if he believes that cleanliness has very little connection to godliness and that constant washing, under the conditions he lives, is too much trouble. He is adamant in his conviction that people are not to be trusted and are not necessary to him, that the news of the outside world, from whatever source, is tainted and false, and that the times of his youth in Sargentville were in every way superior to the present. He is more interested in who will be elected to be his selectman and game warden than he is in his representatives in Washington or the president.

The other day I waved to Kenny when I drove to the post office, reluctant to break my silence by giving him a ride. I need not have worried. The next morning (it was the second day of a cold month) he gestured that he wanted a ride. I stopped for him, and he rode to the post office with me, saying nothing until he got out at his house, under one of the KEEP OUT signs. "Social Security day," he said in his thick, almost incomprehensible Maine accent. Holding his letter of the month, he said good-bye and walked off, a great, slow bear of a man ambling into his cabin.

When I got back to my place, the Captain White House, as it was still called before we moved in, I thought about Kenny. To the summer people of Sargentville, he is a "character" who speaks a strange tongue and looks very much alone and odd. They do not associate themselves with him, because, of course, they lead their lives differently.

But the more I thought about him, the more I realized that he and I are more alike than we are like our other neighbors. I too prefer my own society, I too have become distrustful of what I hear on the TV, the radio, in the newspaper, and do not often listen to them, or read it. We are alike in our critical views of the contemporary world and its inhabitants; we both keep better track of the small animals we live among than the human beings around us. It may be that we part company in our views of personal sanitation. But then it is easy for me, possessed of unlimited hot water, a washing machine and dryer, a shower and a tub, to stay clean. Left to myself without these amenities, I think I would decide that, living alone without a companion or much company, I did not need to worry about clean clothes or baths. Who knows, I might even put up some KEEP OUT signs to replace the discreet PRIVATE one that now stands at the side of my driveway.

❧ ON all the roads I traveled in this very cold, wet, and snowy winter there were warning signs. Some read FROST HEAVE, others simply BUMP. The roads freeze, melt a little, and then freeze again, leaving serious barriers to progress. Being an inattentive driver, I often failed to see the signs and then was jolted out of my driving reveries by hitting the heave, hard. *Then* I was alert, watching for the next BUMP sign. The lesson was: words are not as powerful as acts. Show, do not tell.

❧ A CATALOG came in the mail at the end of an unproductive morning, from Daedalus, a company that supplies bookstores with remainders. It was addressed to Sybil, of course, for she does all the ordering of such books for our single remainder table at the front door. Nonetheless, I scanned its tightly printed pages to find out which of my friends' and acquaintances' works were being cavalierly disposed of for sale (cheaply) in new bookstores, and some old-book stores, like ours.

How self-centered we writers are. Anxiously I first

looked to see if *my* book was remaindered, if Joe's or Bill's or Ellen's or Pete's. . . . The good thing about the catalog is that it does not tell which printing of the book is being emptied out of the publishers' warehouse. So charity allowed me to believe that John's book was in its fifth printing when it was placed on remainder tables in drug- and chain stores, not its first.

I realized how much more I was aware of my vices (envy, gloating, egotism) when I was alone. In the presence of others, it was possible to ignore them, or even deny that they existed. In solitude, they are there, omnipresent and bountiful, unable to be dispelled by the unknowing flattery of kindly others.

❧ HARRY, a kind neighbor and friend, came to the door at three in the afternoon yesterday. Was I OK? Did I need anything? He said he had not seen me about after the big snow storm and wondered how I was getting on. Did I need more wood from the pile across the driveway? Groceries? Company?

Nothing, thank you, I told him, disturbed by the interruption and yet I was tempted to ask him in for coffee and, yes, for his company. But I didn't. I thought of explaining my experiment to him but decided against it, thinking it would sound foolish, even somewhat mad. I thanked him again and closed the door, having preserved my solitude a while longer even as I was aware that I was not eager to.

Jessamyn West (*Hide and Seek*): "The prohibition against solitude is forever. A Carry Nation rises in every person when he thinks he sees someone sneaking off to be alone. It is not easy to be solitary unless you are also born ruthless. Every solitary repudiates someone."

The rebel against solitude arose in me when Harry appeared at the door. I realized that I was not so sure about my desire to be alone. And I was surprised by my willingness (fought off reluctantly) to have company. Perhaps I was not so good at living this way as I believed.

❧ PRAYER: Deciding to say Evening Prayer at the end of my days alone in addition to the Morning Prayers I had always read, I found a short prayer at the back of the *Book of Common Prayer* that I loved, and learned, and said aloud every night as I lay in bed looking across the whitened and featureless cove and the frozen reach: "O Lord, support me all the day long, until the shadows lengthen, and the evening comes, and the busy world is hushed, and the fever of life is over, and my work is done. Then in thy mercy grant me a safe lodging, and a holy rest, and peace at the last."

Those were wonderful phrases—shadows lengthen, the fever of life over, the world hushed, work done, holy rest. Unlike so many other prayers, not hallowed names, kingdoms to come, and grace, righteousness, the power and glory forever and ever, the resurrection and the life; but instead safe lodging and peace at the last.

For days I considered the secular and earthly contents of the prayer. I thought about Simone Weil who wrote a profound essay on the nature of the Lord's Prayer. Should I be granted the boon of knowing when my last day on earth comes, I hoped I would have the strength (and the memory) to say it to myself, over and over, until the last moment.

Thinking of Simone Weil, the saintly Jewish philosopher who hesitated on the threshold of Christianity, I took down my copy of *Gravity and Grace* which she wrote almost fifty years ago. With the kind of luck that had marked most of my reading during the fifty days, I opened to this: "Do not allow yourself to be imprisoned by any affection. Keep your isolation. The day, if it ever comes when you are given true affection, there will be no opposition between interior solitude and friendship, quite the reverse."

This was reassuring to come upon. Not *any* affection but true affection (which I was parted from for the time being but hoped to return to when my walkabout was over) was not likely to disturb the interior solitude I cherished and feared, in a way, to abandon.

❧ A NOTE from Molly Sholes who owns a blueberry farm in Rockport reminded me that when she was visiting us here she was the ideal early-morning guest. She came downstairs in her bathrobe, nodded to me as I sat reading at the kitchen table, took a cup of coffee from the Braun maker, and went silently upstairs to her bedroom to think and do paperwork for her second, elective job as selectman for her town, she told me later. There was something almost holy about the silence of early morning. It became even better when, without discussing it, it was shared by a house guest.

❧ A DAY began with a fine winter sunrise, a long view of the distant horizon slowly taking on color, the sky growing brilliant with yellow streaks transmuted into red, even a royal purple. As I watched, the fully lighted blue-and-white day arrived and the pale yellow-from-sun snow shone like polished ivory. This was the way every good day began. Inevitably the coffee tasted better than it had on a morning full of fog and then snow, and words arrived on the page with some ease, even occasional grace.

The evening always managed to continue the benign sense that the sunrise had provided. There were still possibilities left over for the dark hours. I took my rather sparse dinner (vegetables, rice, and chunks of canned pineapple) into the television room to watch a wonderful Danish film, *Babette's Feast*, sent to me by a son-in-law, Bob Emerson, who was concerned for my sanity, I supposed, in this period of solitude. I loved the film. Even the elegance of the Parisian food that Babette provided for her country employers did not make my pedestrian supper seem insufficient.

In cities where I spent my young days, I was unaware of the power the sunrise could generate. Usually I slept through it, but had I not, I still would have been unable to see it, sunk down as I usually was in second- or fourth-floor apartments. But here I celebrated the whole process throughout the day and well into the evening, when often it would have been reinforced by the might of a blood-red sunset. The thought of their combined glory tinged the events of thirteen hours, lasted by coloring the invisible air in the house red and orange and yellow and purple, suffused it with the pleasure of feeling alive once again.

In solitude I felt the humane force of the sun rising and setting, the temperature, atmosphere, weather. Nothing came between them and me. Nothing, and no one with me, was required to increase (or, if everything was dim, sunless, dark, and uncharitably frozen, decrease) my inner felicity, the climate of my at-peace spirit.

SYBIL wrote to me that she had read Paul Auster's *New York Trilogy* and was delighted with it and at the same time confused by it. She decided not to read the next Auster volume we had stacked up (our mutual habit was to celebrate writers we liked by reading everything we could find by them) but to slip instead into an old Rex Stout Nero Wolfe book. She wrote that she liked the idea of clearing her heated literary palate with the sorbet of a cooling mystery before going on to the next serious work.

ONE late afternoon, in the midst of a heavy snowstorm, twelve inches of a predicted two feet having already fallen and the power having momentarily gone off, I stood in the center of the house and heard the absolute silence. It reminded me of what someone told me Samuel Beckett had said in an interview when he was asked what one of his plays meant. "Don't look for meaning in the words. Listen to the silences."

The music in the pause or the significant rest in John Cage's compositions, the long-held stillness choreographed into the middle of whirling ballet steps, the black, still places of a Francis Bacon color-filled painting in which a faceless figure sits in darkness, seeming to have been exhausted, almost obliterated, into silence, the inner light that is able to shine for the Quakers only when the human voice is quieted, the meaningful dashes between words or phrases or sentences in the poetry of Emily Dickinson representing sound ceasing: all these are heard or seen even when nothing is spoken or painted.

But then again: Absolute silence becomes noisy. This I learned standing in the middle of a quiet room in a quiet house while, like a curtain, the silent snow fell at every window. I heard all that quiet. It made noise.

❧ DISCOVERY: I found that the more suitable form of reading matter, in solitude, was poetry. Lyrics especially. Their length and the single cry of their message suited my relatively short attention span that was characteristic of the *long* time span available to me living alone. Why this was so I could not determine. It might be that time offered me too many possibilities for what I might do: I could not concentrate for long on one thing.

I was not entirely sure of the meaning of Yvor Winters's early poem, "Song," but I liked it well enough to copy it out and then read it again and again throughout one stormy morning. To run before oneself from silence only to fall into an even better silence. To paraphrase Gertrude Stein, if anything means anything, this means something, but I was not sure exactly what. I thought the ambiguity lay in the image of running before oneself. But the little poem proved interesting and stimulating for half a day, surely proof of my theory about poetry.

❧ IN A learned book about words, word-play, and speech (by Peter Farb), I discovered an interesting fact. Throughout their lives the Paliyans of southern India speak very little. By the age of forty they are silent. Those in their community who continue to speak are considered abnormal, "their behavior offensive."

I thought about Ezra Pound who was jailed in an insane asylum after World War II for his fascistic and anti-Semitic broadcasts to the United States. After his release he returned to Italy where, until his death many years later, he spoke very seldom.

To many people his was a mysterious silence. One critic thought he had realized his widely aired political views had been his downfall so he resolved to speak no more. Others believed his silence was due to an acute depression. But in an interview he gave late in his life he hinted at an explanation. Asked why he had stopped all the activities of his productive seventy-seven years, he said: "I don't work anymore. I don't do anything, I have become illiterate and unread. I simply fall into lethargy . . . and I contemplate."

He told her: "One strange day . . . words became void of meaning."

Two years later he said: "I did not enter silence; silence captured me."

One evening, at the house of an acquaintance, Pound was silent. He heard his mistress, Olga Rudge, say that they ought to go home. "We'll never get there," he replied. He said good-bye to his host and asked him: "Why is it that one always happens to be where one does not want to be?"

His daughter, Mary Rudge, thought he spoke when he had something significant to say. She said: "I guess about the best thing [for him] to do is to keep silent" when people asked him silly questions. The silence was "the most wonderful thing that ever happened to him. Silence is an easy etiquette."

Olga Rudge thought his silence was due to his age. "Old people become increasingly silent."

Natalie Barney gave a party for his eightieth birthday. Pound said nothing all evening. Barney thought he had been "an eloquent listener."

Samuel Beckett called on Pound late in his life. Humphrey Carpenter (in whose excellent biography of Pound I found all these accounts) writes: "The two of them had sat together in complete silence for a while. Then Beckett, suddenly able to bear it no longer, got to his feet, embraced Ezra and let himself out of the house." Carpenter called them "the two masters of silence."

One of Pound's psychiatrists used a typical medical euphemism to describe his silence: it was a "retardation of verbal expression."

In my own silence I often thought about Ezra Pound. I decided that, contrary to what I had thought was the chattering practices of most old people, his silence was the more acceptable mode. It represented contemplation, as he said. I think it is entirely possible that a good critic, like Pound, would look back on his creative work as insufficient, "botched," "a mess" (these were his terms when he was asked about the *Cantos*), not because it *was* but because, in hindsight, it never approached what the poet hoped it would be, thought it might be at the time. So, having written and talked so much for so long, he chose silence as the way of self-criticism. Present silence was a way of saying no to the past. I understood this.

It was also a mode of behavior in which he could discover the truths about himself, an investigation Pound may have been forced into by his imprisonment and later by his ruined life in Italy. Perhaps there was too little time during his early life of fame and acclaimed achievement to conduct this search. Later in his life he was given the time, unpleasantly, it is true, but still. . . . In those last years he listened, eloquently, instead of talking eloquently. Having mastered his poetic idiom, he abandoned it to master silence. There was resistance to the people and the world around him in this: He was a "quiet rebel."

❧ EVER since their founding by George Fox more than

three centuries ago, the Quakers have had little faith in speech. In their eyes much talk is a sign of worldliness and a detriment to direct communion with God. During their worship service they sit silent for long periods of time to make way for direct conversation with the Holy Spirit, and the reception of an inner light. They are a notable exception among worshipers who traditionally evolve an elaborate spoken ritual to embody the tenets and practice of their faith.

In many ways, I found, the Friends understood. God seemed closer to me during the rare, short periods of silence in the Episcopal rite. When I prayed alone in the morning and evening, God seemed nearby or at least available to my unspoken words. Without the distractions of other persons, without the extraneous sounds of their voices and my own, I felt the presence of God's absence, to paraphrase Paul Valéry, not a noisy landscape of the mind but a still life.

IN A landscape of snow and bare trees, I stood on the deck at noon, already tired and unusually aware of the black trunk of the scrub oak and the charcoal limbs of the poplars down the path. There was nothing left of these testaments to winter-death but their skeletons. I thought of the book I owned of photographs by Frank Horvat (*The Tree*, text by John Fowles) in which muted beeches (*faux de verzy*) in France, blooming ocotillo with no evident blooms, and the green twisted bare limbs of oaks in California, the wiry, bare lime trees in Derbyshire, England,

Apple Tree, December, Zurich, Switzerland,
from The Tree *by John Fowles. Photographs and preface copyright © 1979 by Frank Horvat. By permission of Little, Brown and Company.*

stand in undistinguished, flat landscapes, reminding me of murdering winters in which only time and spring can effect a resurrection.

My city-loving daughter, Barbara, once told me she did not wish to live in the country because, she said mockingly, she was afraid of trees. At these moments in the dead of winter (an accurate phrase: the dead of winter) I too was afraid of their unnatural, stiff lifelessness, their black anatomies without the softness of leaves. They terrorized me with their stationary and implacable threat. Every vestige of their former autumnal glory, and their lush, summer fullness, was gone. Their present was somehow ominous and intimidating. I had forgotten their past. It was beyond re-creation, and I could not believe in the possibility of it.

The music I listened to every afternoon began to take on the semblance of menace. When I felt most desolate, the heavy tones of Richard Strauss's *Four Last Songs* (*Vier Letzte Lieder*), the weary, tender words of one of them, "Im Abendrot" ("At Sunset") by Joseph von Eichendorff, in the isolation of my sitting room seemed far more poignant than when I had heard Jessye Norman sing them at the Kennedy Center to an audience of almost a thousand persons. Alone here, her huge voice on a compact disc, carefully reduced to its softest and most eloquent contralto level, brought me to the edge of tears. It was unbearable to hear the gentle sadness and resignation of

> Vom Wandern ruhen wir
> *We are resting from our wandering*

Nun überm stillen Land.
now above the quiet countryside.

Bald ist es Schlafenzeit,
Soon it will be time to sleep,
Das wir uns night verirren
lest we lose our way
In dieser Einsamkeit.
in this solitude.

O weiter, stiller Friede.
O broad, deep peace.
So tief im Abendrot,
So deep in the sunset,
Wie sind wir wandermüde—
how tired of wandering we are—
Ist dies etwa der Tod?
could this perhaps be death?

The words were not Strauss's, but the music came from a very old man, a year before his death to which he seemed to be entirely resigned. The quiet countryside, the solitude of wandering and sleep, the peace of the dying sun, were all intimations of death, or, the poet Joseph von Eichendorff asked, were they death itself?

Music like this is better heard among people, as part of an audience. I made a decision to choose my afternoon selections more carefully, seeking out the sunnier arias from Mozart operas or the Goldberg variations or the early Beethoven quartets.

❧ I TURNED the page of the desk calendar to a new month and came upon another daunting Edward Hopper painting, *Approaching a City.* Many-storied buildings with regular, empty windows occupy the top half. Cutting them off midway is an off-white wall ending in a blue-black empty tunnel. At the bottom are two sets of railroad tracks disappearing into the tunnel and appearing to be approaching infinity, coming to a single point just beyond the end of the canvas.

In the painting there are no persons, no motion, nothing but static facades of buildings, walls, lines of tracks, and the cave of darkness into which nothing comes or goes: the ultimate representation of urban solitude, hard-edged isolation, unending inhuman structures, and implied human loneliness, for some arcane reason, although no person is present.

I learned that there is a softness about being alone in the country, even the frozen, snow-filled country. Solidity, concrete, and bricks do not define one's surroundings. The edges of my landscape are blurred, made uneven by the action of wind and bending branches. There is a comforting balm in the way the water beyond the white meadow breaks through the ice when the tide comes in and then freezes over in irregular ridges when it goes out.

The city is a multitude of rigid right angles forced down upon each other. But the country, even in the dead of winter, is composed of the circles and arcs and ovals of blessedly unpopulated, almost empty space.

Most of Hopper's canvases are exterior, so it was always a wonder that his pictures suggest to me interior states of

Edward Hopper's Approaching a City *(1946). Oil on canvas, 27⅛ × 36 inches (68.9 × 91.4 cm.). Courtesy of the Phillips Collection, Washington, D.C.*

Francis Bacon's Study of Figure in a Landscape *(1952).*
Oil on canvas, 78 × 54¼ inches (198.1 × 137.7 cm.).
Courtesy of the Phillips Collection, Washington, D.C.

heart-stopping loneliness, never serenity or peace. In an unexpected flash of memory, I recalled that, in the early seventies, I saw a painting at the Phillips Collection in Washington, D.C., that haunted me for more than twenty years: Francis Bacon's *Study of Figure in a Landscape*. I saw it again when the Hirshhorn Museum housed a large exhibition of Bacon's work in 1989. The figure appears to be kneeling in a field high with what may be hay. He may be nude—I cannot tell for sure—and his shadow is black against the yellow hay behind him. In the background there are trees, slightly more colored than the foreground, but not much. A patch of ominous blue sky with clouds the color, almost, of the hay and the trees darkens the figure.

There was something frightening, terrible, about him, perhaps because he crouches down, nude, in a field, while almost every other figure in the exhibition of paintings was indoors. He appears to be at the mercy of his undifferentiated surroundings and, at the same time, to be threatening the spectator. He is more alone than I was now remembering him, and when I found the catalog I could not bear to look at him for long.

❧ FEELING overwhelmed by what Simone Weil called "interior solitude," I took a walk along the icy path to the beach, clinging for dear life to my cane in one hand, my pointed stick in the other. The snow was a perilous disguise for the hard crust that covered the grass, the field, and then the pebbled shore, as though the earth had shrunk into its elderly self leaving this skin of ice to protect it. I felt threatened by every step. Wherever I looked there was nothing but hard white surfaces and featureless whitened trees.

Our small portion of the cove was filled with wrinkled floes, heaped up in layers, the only break in the frozen water. As the tide moved there was the sharp crackling noise of protesting cakes of ice being moved slightly by still-fluid water. No other sound that I could hear, no protesting sea birds, nothing but the cold shell of the earth forbidding all movement, and the deafening silence of being even more alone, in the frozen cove, than I had been in the warm house.

In those cold days, I noticed that I found it hard to recall the names of persons I had met up here for the first time. I tried to fix names to faces I dimly remembered, and occupations or home towns to names. But they had all faded quickly. I now understood the truth about the elderly: the persons of one's younger days adhere to one's memory permanently, but newcomers rarely find a foothold. I could hold onto fictional characters, observations of the world around me, ideas, conjectures, and questions about the quality of my life alone. But recent acquaintances? Not one of them could be retrieved from my failing memory to populate my solitude.

There was one exception. Four years ago, when I first came to live in Sargentville, I learned that the novelist and editor Helen Yglesias lived eight miles away in Brooklin. I left a message on her answering machine saying I would like to meet her. She called back. We arranged to meet here for tea.

At once we formed a strong connection, composed of the many parallels in our lives. We were almost the same age and had both grown up in New York, albeit in separate boroughs, she in the Bronx, I in Manhattan. We shared memories of that remarkable city, especially Greenwich Village. In almost the same years we edited the literary sections of magazines. Late in our lives we began to write fiction. By the time we met we had published about the same number of books, written criticism for the same periodicals and newspapers, taught at the same writers' workshop, and resided at the same writers' colonies. We both had successful grown children and young grandchildren; we were both divorced.

Curiously, we had never encountered each other before. She had come to Maine long before I had. But fortunately for me, we were here now, and again fortunately, an unusual occurrence for me, late in life, we had become friends.

Helen became a tie to the literary world from which, what with age and distance, I had become somewhat dissassociated. She knew more people in publishing and kept her connections to them by spending part of each winter in New York. Recently she had lost her best friend, the poet Eve Merriam, to death from cancer and was still mourning her absence. More recently, she had hoped to fill her loneliness up here by having an older sister come to live with her. But it had not worked out. Her sister had gone back to live in Florida, having found Maine too isolated, too cold, too lacking in the amenities of city and in friends of her own age. Shortly after she returned to Miami, she became ill, and Helen went down to care for her.

Helen and I stayed in touch with each other by mail. She wrote about the artificiality of my experiment, pointing out that, since I knew it would have a certain end, I could not understand what the prospect of unbroken loneliness was. She said she was now more occupied than ever, having learned that another, elder sister, who also lived in Florida, was ill. She was planning to go to see her.

She said she longed for some solitude. Her plight reminded me of Edith Wharton writing about Lily Barth in *The House of Mirth:* "She was not accustomed to taste the joys of solitude except in company."

❧ Two and one-half weeks into what I began to think of as the winter of my content, I felt the strange stirrings of material. Writers are entirely egocentric. To them, few things in their lives have meaning or importance unless they give promise of serving some creative purpose. They waste nothing they hear or feel or see or are told; nothing is lost on them, as Henry James observed.

So I began to record, on odd pieces of paper, backs of envelopes, and torn memo-pad sheets, what I was learning about being alone. I felt it was all too insignificant, too scrappy, to put into a bound notebook. But still. . . . What had at first been enriching and sustaining as I lived it, became, well, subject matter. I found I was living, listening, thinking, watching, in order to have something to *write*, in much the same way, I had always thought, that Hemingway went to wars, fishing, and big-game hunting in order to write novels about them. For me, however, it was a mistake, I decided. This was wrong. What I put down should always come from the rich roil of the past, from the memory and the storage bins of the mind, never from the experiences of the moment. So I stopped writing about being alone, I *was* alone, and that was enough for the present.

I went back to writing fiction.

❧ EVERYWHERE I traveled on a round of chores during the coldest day we had had all winter—the post office, the general store, the gas station, the new-books store, the library to donate review copies, the hardware store to buy melting crystals—I was the only customer there. *The only one there!* I thought of the crowded city I had left behind, the lines to the check-out, the lines at the movie theater, the people in cities who are not only there but who pushed me from behind, from all sides. I was relieved that I had escaped to this peninsula, even though the temperature when I left the house was twenty below.

❧ I HAVE never been a saver of things, like Sybil. As quickly as I can I throw away whatever I cannot use at the moment. But small things, reminiscent of places I have visited or lived, cling to me without my noticing them. Until last week when, to my surprise, I found an old matchbox hidden under a wooden candlestick. IOWA HOUSE was printed on its cover, a place I had not stayed in eighteen years. Then, having nothing better to do on an early evening (which started at four in the afternoon), I went through a pen-and-pencil holder in the kitchen and discovered an old, small, red automatic pencil with ALBANY ACADEMY on its side in gilt. Why had I never noticed it before in the twenty years since I lived in Albany and sent my daughters to the sister school of the academy?

And in the same week, searching for scrap paper in a stack of old pads I came upon a neat, blue-printed one that read: DEPARTMENT OF STATE and under it, in smaller letters, The Secretary. I must have picked it up twenty years ago to take notes when the editors of the *New Republic* were invited to an off-the-record lunch with Henry Kissinger. It was, I believe, in March 1974. I can't remember much of what the Secretary of State said in that State Department dining room. But I still had the pad.

And, again in the same week: Out of my copy of Elizabeth Bowen's *To the North*, which I read when I was in Bellagio fifteen years ago, there fell the Villa Serbelloni bookplate. How did it get there? Why did it choose to show itself in the week in which all the other memorabilia appeared? What were they all saying to me about the insistent role of the past in the life I was now leading? Were they demanding some kind of autobiographical recognition, an acknowledgment in fiction or memoir? Or was it accident,

Villa Serbelloni bookplate.

the detrital reminder of times and places, for some reason I wished to forget, the debris of dead matter in a dead season?

❧ LATE one night—it might have been two in the morning but, being alone, the exact or proper time for doing anything mattered not at all to me—I started a new section of the novel, feeling much inflated and proud of myself to be able to work at an hour I was usually asleep. Henry James called fiction "the balloon of experience," a wonderful phrase which, that night, described not only the fiction but the fiction writer.

❧ ON A day of absolute nonproduction, a day as blank inside as the white stretches of covered ground outside my study window, I began to wonder if white was the color of creative drought. I made the trek through the snow to the bookstore to find on the wall a framed quotation from Paul Valéry:

> The truth is that every sheet of blank paper by its very emptiness affirms that nothing is as beautiful as what does not exist. In the magic mirror of its white expanse the soul beholds the setting where signs and lines will bring forth miracles. This presence of absence both spurs on and, at the same time, paralyzes the pen's commitment. . . .

This came from his essay "La Feuille Blanche." Finding it

saved the pallid day for me. Imbued with the presence of absence I suddenly felt occupied and productive. I had been paralyzed by a lack of ideas, but now I saw that I did not need to produce anything on the page to feel better, even, somehow, complete. What I did not produce was, to Valéry's way of thinking, more beautiful than anything I could have written. Nothing was more comforting than to have remembered dimly, and then found, Valéry's words on the wall of Wayward Books.

❧ JUDE BARTLETT, the handsome young dancer who died of AIDS this winter, a few miles away in Brooklin, continued to haunt my solitude. Having been so close to his dying, I kept expecting to hear of the sickening and then death of others I knew were afflicted with the same terrible plague.

I remembered that Emily Dickinson wrote to a friend: "I notice where Death has been introduced, he frequently calls." This turned out to be prophetic for me. Two days later I had word from Allan Gurganus that an old acquaintance from Yaddo days, the artist David Vereano, had died, at forty-four. I could still see him clearly, seated on a low stool on a hill above Saratoga Springs, wearing his wide Walt Whitman hat, his handsome smile and Egypt-tinted skin shining in the half-sunlight he loved to paint. I remembered how much of his canvases were sky and clouds; I thought of him now as elevated to his beloved empyrean, having risen above the horizon to become another himself. This was as it should be.

❧ THE radio reported a storm on the way from the south. The weather bureau broadcast a WINTER STORM WATCH. I battened everything down, and waited. Then the announcement was changed to WINTER STORM WARNING. Obediently I watched as it approached, blackening the sky over Deer Isle and then lowering itself, it seemed to me, over my roof, singling me out for its largest delivery of snow. The heavy-flaked snow fell straight down all evening, all night, and the next morning, until the heralded WINTER STORM diminished into flurries and passed on to the north. It had made no noise, no wind created drifts. It left behind a flat, high landscape and a greater silence than I had heard before, a welcome isolation, for the moment, from roads and the desire for outward-bound excursions.

While listening for reports of the storm's progress, I heard part of a story about the newly elected president who, it was said, was a saxophone player and a lover of jazz. All I caught was that, as a young boy, he had thought the name of the great jazz pianist Thelonius Monk was The Loneliest Monk.

❧ "SHARE." "Sharing." "I want to share with you." The fine thing about being alone was that the whole odious concept of sharing completely disappeared. For one, there was no one to share *with*. Quickly, my desire "to share," never very strong at best, died away. I found pleasure in storing up, *saving* what I realized and saw and thought, like a miser, like a squirrel.

Somewhere else I have put down what I thought about the conversationalist who begins by saying, "Let me share with you my experiences. . . ." At once, I recoil, knowing that this is to be a long, tedious monologue and not, as the word means, an exchange of something we have in common. What has become of the honest, direct, Old English word "tell" (*tellan*, to relate)? When someone on the radio, as it happened one morning during my weeks alone, announced she was going to share with me her views on . . . I cut her off, and went back to the blessedness of the vacant space where there is no need for unburdening.

❧ WHEN I lived in cities, surrounded on every side by people, served by them constantly, I never knew the names of the person who sold newspapers at the corner, delivered them to the door in the early hours of the morning, collected the garbage, waited on me in the grocery store, delivered UPS packages and the mail. Rarely did I see their faces, or if I did, they were still, somehow, invisible, a part of the anonymous fog of the overpopulation that pushed in upon me from every side.

Here, now, I knew the names and life histories of everyone who had ever come to the house, to plow after snowstorms, to put up gutters and rototill the garden, to mow down the meadow and to fix the plumbing, the electricity, the telephone, the antenna, and the steps. While I was alone I thought of them as I looked at the work they had done to this old house and for this old person. I felt grateful to the now-invisible community that had provided me with workable systems and support, to everyone out there who would come if I called for help: "Hello, Sven, my antenna has blown down in last night's wind. Could you . . . ?" Or, as happened one day: "Hello, Mr. Byard. I'm in Sargentville. My car won't start [it had been twenty-two below the night before]. Could you . . . ?"

Danny, who bakes our bread, buns, doughnuts, pies, and cakes, lives down the road, does his work behind the general store less than a mile away, and sells from its counter. He is a Beatles devotee and comes by the bookstore in summer to buy whatever books Sybil can find for him. I liked this, this was part of my definition of community: the baker, the Beatles, his bread, all part of it. In this sense I belong to the much-maligned Middle Ages which I studied as a graduate student, to a time when villages were sufficient communities and people knew, served, and relied upon each other.

I thought about the implications of "community" when I was alone. It is easy to live apart among these known, named persons. Our lives impinge upon each other at tangential points of necessity. Yet it was hard to feel part of a community when I lived in New York or Washington.

❧ PLANNING: The days grew shorter, until there were only nine hours of light. Boundaries that others usually placed upon my time disappeared, leaving me with edgeless days (though short) and seemingly endless nights. So I found that plans were useless. To plan a day began to mean to start out into it, and then to find myself on many unexpected tangents from the forward progress, the main-

stream of the plan. The digressions—what I did that I had no idea I would do—turned out to be more interesting.

Example: I sat at the computer, resolved to put two manuscript pages of fiction into the machine. By accident my eyes lit on a bookmark from Pomegranate Press that had fallen out of a book by Israel Rosenfield I once started and then left unfinished. The bookmark had a long, startling photograph (from the archives of the Library of Congress) of Dr. Mary Edwards Walker, a physician and reformer during Civil War years and who, the text of the bookmark informed me, objected to the "stricture" of nineteenth-century women's clothing.

So there she was, in tails and rather baggy black trousers, a silk vest, dress shirt, and black tie, holding her high silk hat in her white-gloved hand. An invisible timepiece hung from a gold chain around her neck and was tucked into her vest pocket. A medal was pinned to the left side of her formal jacket. Her gray-white hair was cut short and lay straight down behind her very large, protruding ears. Her face was ordinary, almost androgynous; her slightly sunken smile suggested a possible absence of teeth.

Dr. Walker was a wondrous sight to behold, especially when I remembered the customary ladies' crinolines of her day. So I made my way through high snow to the locked-up bookstore. In the tomblike cold I found some reference books and looked up her history. She was born in 1832, studied medicine at Syracuse Medical College, and

Dr. Mary Edwards Walker (1832–1919).
Photograph courtesy of the Library of Congress.

graduated as a surgeon when she was twenty-three. Ten years later she offered her services to the Union Army as a surgeon but was rejected because of her sex. So she joined as a nurse and served three years before she was finally commissioned an assistant surgeon. Near the end of the war she was awarded the Congressional Medal of Honor which she wore at all times on her male clothes for the rest of her life. She died in 1919, at the age of eighty-seven.

There is a biography of Mary Walker, published in 1962. At the end of the morning I called the local library to see if interlibrary loan could produce it for me. The librarian said she would try. I was so full of questions that I thought about her for the rest of the day. What was the effect of her determinedly antifeminine dress upon the people she doctored? Was she too old to serve in the Spanish-American War? World War I? Did she marry? Have children? Was she celibate? Or lesbian? Where did she practice, at what hospital, in what city?

So deep into imaginings and questions that the meander wiped out the mainstream of my plan, I never got back to the computer.

ONCE I had a character in a novel who had been a silent-picture star. He grew old living alone, his close friends having died. The film industry had moved into irrevocable, omnipresent sound. But he believed that the art of silence was greater than the ubiquitous spoken word and accompanying music. His loneliness was made more bearable by alcohol and by the imaged presence in his room of a stationary old camera. It sat on three legs, had a crank at the side which turned the loop of film, and a black box housing the lens which could be moved from side to side.

My character, Willis Lord, would place himself before the camera. He imagined it was recording his actions as he cooked, or washed, or prepared for bed. His sense of his status as a star, a person at the center of every action, was thus maintained during his long, solitary days and nights.

In an odd way, when I was alone, this fiction became predictive. At moments when I went through the ordinary acts of daily life, I too imagined the presence of a camera, a more modern, mobile, hand-held one, I suppose, that followed me everywhere. I was not conscious of another person operating the camera, merely the camera moving on its own in a pair of hands, giving a curious significance to my every move.

I had an eerie sense of having been dichotomized, myself split into two, one acting, the other watching and recording for some higher purpose. But what? To make sure I was doing normal things? What I was supposed to be doing? I wondered if we were all always observing ourselves, even as we slept? Or did it happen only when we were alone, or most often in the late years of our lives when we had grown fearful of diminishment? When we were young we knew what we were doing, but now, did we need a witness to record any deviation from our youthful selves?

I had no answers. I knew only that when I raised the shades in the bedroom each morning, the camera was there, watching to see if I succeeded in making them exactly level, if my eye was still accurate, my hand steady, my memory firm. At once, I was one with old Willis Lord and my old self, one and the same, and the camera was the second person singular, judge, censor, arbiter, and critic.

☙ THE month and a half I spent alone was the time of the first days of the Clinton administration. But politics played no part in my thinking. I had no newspaper delivered, the TV was down. My source of news was National Public Radio via a Maine station in Bangor to which I listened for twenty minutes at six o'clock in the morning and twenty in the late afternoon.

I turned off all commentators on the air and I talked to no one about the political situation by telephone. These self-imposed conditions may account for my conviction that what was going on out there in the world was, inevitably, unthinkable, and that I ought to preserve my hard-achieved peace of mind by banning even the forty minutes I had hitherto indulged in.

I used to be certain that writers needed to be *au courant* about everything that went on in the world of their time. This is probably good advice for the first fifty or sixty years they live. But later, I decided, I wanted to shield myself from as much of the terrible particulars of modern existence as possible to preserve my shrinking time for, well, let me say it, pompous as it sounds, contemplation of more important questions, of generalities based on a past I have stored away for review in the leisure of an elderly present.

The horrifying details of life in the world today, of rape, wars, AIDS, starvation, assassinations, murders, drugs, floods, hurricanes, torture, abuse of women and children, racism, drunkenness, madness, homelessness, political chicanery could not be buried or wished away by an act of will, certainly. But they were held at arm's length for the short period I had devoted to the exploration of solitude.

Without their constant presence, my mind appeared to be a long, low, insensate, featureless plain. It contained no peaks of drama and no deep troughs of despair. It had been leveled by the temporary absence of the world beyond my own integument. In that state I felt somewhat barren but still comfortable, an arboreal intellectual sloth who could think but not feel very much. I was not stirred by indignation or repelled by sanguinity. "In violence we forget who we are," Mary McCarthy wrote. Without the constant presence of violence in my consciousness I knew who I was. And, for short periods of time, that was enough.

PAUL VALÉRY wrote one novel, *Monsieur Teste*. The man of the title is a severely introverted man living alone in a city with his wife. I phrase this last clause deliberately because Madame Teste (or anyone else) plays no part whatever in Teste's consciousness or in his unending search for the contents of his thoughts. He is a man who limits himself and his existence to his mind or, as Valéry writes, "a man regulated by his own powers of thought." He is friendless except for Valéry who wrote the book from his memory of his own "inward youth" while he was searching "in myself for the critical points in my powers of attention." He had wanted to be able "to extend the duration of certain thoughts."

Most interesting to me, Valéry in those days put away writing in his solitude because "it seemed to me unworthy to divide my ambition between the desire to produce an effect on others and the passion to know and acknowledge myself as I was, without omission, pretense, or complacency." Writing, thus, was an act aimed at impressing others, so it ran counter to his efforts to search for himself.

Early in my fifty days I spent one day and one evening with Monsieur Teste, looking for assistance in my time ahead, alone. Most of the novel contains "snapshots" and "thoughts" from his notebook. They are merely sketched in; few are developed. Like a complex mosaic they compose the mind of the man, enough, Valéry may have thought, to make a novel.

What I found in Monsieur Teste's thinking was of some use to me, if not to act upon, then to ponder:

—"The mind must not be occupied with persons; *de personis non curandum*."

—"What really matters to someone (I mean the kind of someone who in his essence is unique and alone) is precisely that which makes him feel that he is alone. . . . It is this that comes to him when he is *truly alone*, even when in fact he is with others."

—"I am not turned toward the world. My face is to the WALL. There is not an atom of the wall's surface that is not known to me."

—"There are individuals who feel their senses separate them from the real, from being. That sense in them infects their other senses. . . . What I see blinds me. What I hear deafens me. That by which I know makes me ignorant. I am ignorant inasmuch, and insofar, as I know. This light before me is a blindfold and hides either a darkness or a light more. . . . More what? Here the circle of that strange reversal closes: knowledge as a cloud over being; the bright world as an opaque growth on the eye. . . . Away from everything, so that I may see."

—THE MAN OF GLASS: "So direct is my vision, so pure my sensation, so clumsily complete my knowledge, and so quick, so clear my reflection, and my understanding so perfect, that I see through myself from the farthest end of the world down to my unspoken word; and from the shapeless *thing* desired on waking, along the known nerve fibers and organized centers, I *follow* and *am myself*, I answer myself, reflect and reverberate myself, I quiver to the infinity of mirrors—I am glass."

But the best sentence, the one that echoed in my head long after I had put *Monsieur Teste* down: "One must go into himself armed to the teeth."

So it is, truly, I thought, not only armed to the teeth but also wearing a full plate of armor: helmet, beaver, paultron, breastplate, gauntlet, greave, and all the pieces of metal in between. Even so protected, one is still not safe from assault by the guerrilla forces of painful memories and deeply hidden guilt.

❧ I FOUND that when I was alone my hunger grew for opera, live music, ballet, and theater. True, I had a good supply of operas on video and audio tapes and compact discs for music (never the same thing as being at a performance, although at first I thought they would serve). I yearned for the sight of "live" art in galleries and museums.

By good luck, on the day my appetite was greatest, there arrived in the mail a copy of the volume that served as companion to the Barnes Collection exhibition. The handsome book came to Sargentville on the day the exhibition opened in Washington, D.C. I decided to pretend (to what games being alone sometimes drove me!) that I was attending the show, in person, as they say.

Slowly I advanced through the more than three hundred pictures, at least half of them in very good color. I thought I had seen all the Manets, Renoirs, Cézannes, Picassos, Matisses, and Gauguins when I visited the Barnes Museum near Philadelphia many years ago. But I found I had forgotten most of them. Albert Barnes's eccentric decision not to allow his art, in all these years, to be seen away from his museum, made them all seem new to me and wonderfully fresh.

I decided to spend an evening on each painter, to prolong the experience, looking at each picture again and again, thinking about them, and trying to remember them when I came away from the book. My daughter Elizabeth once went to the National Gallery, spent hours in the Impressionist rooms, came back to our house on Capitol

Hill, and amazed us by discussing the pictures she had seen *in the order they hung on the walls.*

I made progress until I came to the early Blue Period Picasso. I don't recall ever seeing *L'ascète* before. Its gaunt, melancholy, starving figure became my companion for days. He is a white-haired man seated before an empty plate, with what appears to be a roll or a piece of bread in his bony fingers, the other hand empty, and a curious blue shadow behind him, possibly his own, but it is not certain. He looks ahead, unseeing, like the blind man in the Metropolitan's picture of the same period, called *The Blind Man's Meal.*

The editor's notes for the picture informed me that Picasso may have been depressed by the suicide of a friend during the four years of his Blue Period. He painted starving and suffering figures, sick and emaciated bodies, sunken faces sad to the point of utter despair. I recognized the universality of *The Ascetic.* Painted ninety years ago, it seemed to me to be prophetic, the open-eyed blindness, the cadaverous, decaying body and almost skeletal head of the old man had the inevitable appearance of a person in the last stages of AIDS. I realized how close to the condition of starvation were the men I had known in the AIDS rooms at Capitol Hill Hospital and my dying friends.

Almost a century ago, under different conditions, Picasso had painted them: the same dire blue-gray skin, the premature aging, the deep-set eyes, and sunken cheeks of the unseeing sufferer, all there, then and now.

Pablo Picasso's The Blue Man *[The Ascetic] (1903).*

❧ FOR the fifth time in my life I read George Eliot's *Middlemarch,* the one novel (together with, perhaps, a late novel by Henry James) I would want to reread were I placed in solitary confinement. With the kind of serendipity I have noted before in these days, I came upon an observation of Eliot's that bore upon my present way of life: "There is no creature whose inward being is so strong that it is not greatly determined by what lies outside it."

Determined = formed? or, directed? But not, I thought, forever. There may be a time, such as now, when the search for the inward being cuts it away from determination by others, frees it for the moment from direction from the outside, gives it stasis, and more than that temporary peace.

Desultory thoughts on solitude:

I noticed that one keeps one's friends better when one is alone. The corollary to this is that one loses one's friends, slowly, when one sees them too often or when they visit for too long a time.

"People who cannot bear to be alone are the worst company" (Albert Guinon).

Inner resources: What are they? Are they like mineral resources, so deeply buried that they require a mining operation to raise them to the surface. Or are they simply *there*, so that they can be used at will, like the ability to follow a line of thought to its conclusion, as the young Valéry trained himself to do, or like the rich muck of memory that yields useful parallels and evidence for one's ideas at the moment they are required, or like the ability to lose oneself in books and be comforted and interested in music and live in paintings, to be able to forget the world and remember only the faint shadow of the inner being one is searching for.

I had closed off all the doors to the house except the one to the flight of steps equipped with roughened treads against the chance of my falling. So I had cut off the many means of egress, and thus the temptation to go out.

My message on the telephone said: "If you must reach me call back after five." I trusted to that gruff sentence to discourage callers. I did not promise to call back because I had no intention of doing so. But of course I knew that if a report of a catastrophe should be left on the answering machine I would return the call at once. The only way to avoid the arrival of bad news would have been to turn off the machine and unplug the telephone.

A church's charity is often known as "outreach." Reaching out. I was trying for a kind of inreach, an "inscape," in Gerard Manley Hopkins's term.

The radio news, in a single day while I was alone: Disastrous floods in southern California. Two trains collide in Gary, Indiana, and six persons are decapitated. One hundred fifty miles from Ankara, Turkey, an entire village is buried in snow. The United States and its allies bomb Iraq, killing many civilians. An Estonian ship breaks up near Finland, spilling two hundred thousand gallons of oil.

Here in Sargentville, on the bank of Billings Cove, two matters of great moment: two grosbeaks arrived at the feeder and the Eggemoggin Reach froze over for the first time in thirty-two years.

After eight hours of silence, I felt dried out, like a well entirely without water. I found myself saying aloud to my computer: "Why are you sitting there mute, doing nothing for me?"

When no thoughts of any value came to me I blamed it on my way of life, not on myself. Margaret Mead believed that "a small group of thoughtful people could change the world. Indeed, it's the only thing that ever has." But what of a person without thoughts? Is she an obstacle to progress and change?

Only for wood, coffee, water, the toilet did I leave my warm study during the sometimes productive hours of the morning. On the way to and from the kitchen I discovered the need to straighten every object and to put on the shelves every displaced book I passed. Was I tidying up all the rooms outside in hopes that then I could make some order out of the scrabbly manuscript on my desk? Or was I putting off returning to the verbal battles in the study, like a soldier recovered from his wounds who dreads returning to the front line?

The house expanded. It now seemed to have more rooms than before, even with three upstairs rooms closed off. I found that the silence I maintained also increased until it filled every space, pushed out the walls, invaded closets, drawers, and cupboards. Eventually it seeped out through the house's seams and surrounded the whole property with a blessed, protective wall of quiet.

The less one talks the more one thinks? Is thought internalized speech rising from and then directed back, soundlessly, into oneself?

Talk uses up ideas, although others have told me that they find it profitable to talk out their ideas and plans for a story because it clarifies their intentions. Not I. Once I have spoken them aloud, they are lost to me, dissipated into the noisy air like smoke. Only if I bury them, like bulbs, in the rich soil of silence do they grow. Sometimes I am lucky. In the interment process, they often multiply and become more complex.

INAUGURATION DAY, January 20, 1993. Sybil had gone to Washington to attend a private party with friends. She had waited twelve years for this change of administration. During that time we held three mourning wakes four years apart on inauguration days. Now it seemed to her only fitting to celebrate.

I stayed at home and listened to some of the events on the radio. Afterward I took a nap. When I woke, still dazed from the force of late afternoon sleep, I fantasized about how Bill Clinton might more suitably have taken office:

In this year of severe recession, unemployment, homelessness, and hunger, he might have announced that, because of great need in the country, there would be no fancy balls (there were thirteen), no limos, no grandstands and parades, no elaborate lunches and dinners. Instead, he would be sworn in on the steps of the Capitol at the usual moment, with his vice president, in the standing presence of everyone who wished to be there. "The Star-Spangled Banner" would be played by the Marine band and sung by the gathering, led by the fine voice of Marilyn Horne. Then Mr. Clinton would return to the White House in a simple American car, perhaps a Ford, to begin the business of the nation "for which I was hired," as he noted earlier in a speech.

The money saved—for transportation, clothing, hairdressing, hotels, overtime police and protection services, limousines, parties, and the extraordinary paraphernalia of parades—might be turned over to the many welfare services now in danger of being cut from the budget, or used to make a small dent in the national debt.

In this way Bill Clinton would be known to history as the first president to put human need before pomp, the first to make significant contributions to the commonweal in place of self-gratifying, empty celebration.

❧ SILENCE and isolation are freeing agents. The chatter

of company, the news of the imperiled and turgid world imprisons me.

I wondered if the sure way into the self is to lose one's senses, totally: to become deaf, blind, without voice, without tactile ability. Under those extreme conditions, perhaps, would the mind be freed to expand without stimulus from anything outside. Would it function on its own?

I read the newspaper in the protection of my silent house. I learned that Senator Daniel Moynihan, a thirty-year expert on welfare, says American society has "normalized" all its worst social ills: teen-aged pregnancy and suicide, divorce, street violence and death, sexual disease, child and wife abuse, drugs, homelessness of the poor and the mad, the enormous black jail population, guns in the grade schools, crimes of every sort. We no longer are indignant about these things. We accept them as normal. They are commonplace, almost unnoticed by some of us.

Marshall McLuhan: "If the temperature of the bath rises one degree every ten minutes, how will the bather know when to scream?"

But I am far from contact with all these terrible, "normal" characteristics of modern society. So I have tended to magnify their importance, to dwell on them with pity and terror. In solitude, they occupy far more of my time than I wish. I would have to go back to living among them, as I once did, to have them become normal to me.

A reluctant interview with the painter ninety-year-old Esteban Vincente, in the *New Yorker*: "My paintings talk, and I don't have anything else to say. I'm still trying to find out what painting is, and the only way to do that is to be alone. The loneliness has to do with what you do."

❧ OFTEN in the late night I dreamed of Jude Bartlett, the young man who died this winter of AIDS in nearby Brooklin. He inhabited my dreams in odd ways, sometimes on his toes in a ballet I could not identify, sometimes holding my hand, once laughing at something I had said. He had been dead some months, but he was often present in my quiet house when I slept, out of his bed and once, curiously, lying beside me in mine.

Jean Hylan, his sister, brought Jude by ambulance from his apartment in New York City to the house she had rented around the corner from where she lived with her husband and five-year-old daughter, Kate. Before she decided to do this, her mother had said to her: "Why don't you put him in a hospital and let professionals take care of him?"

Jean thought otherwise. She organized the community to help with his care. Some people came to sit with him and provide for his almost constant needs, others cooked or shopped. Still others stayed the night to spare Jean the cost of too many health-care professionals. A nurse came on occasion to change his IVs and dress his sores. But most of the ordinary work was done by people who had never before had contact with a gay man suffering the last terrible afflictions of AIDS.

Jude was a gentle, sweet fellow who had been a dancer with the Martha Graham troupe and then a chef. He was still concerned about his appearance and disturbed about his decaying and fallen-out teeth. Although Jean was aware that he had very little time left, she had a dentist visit him to fit him with a bridge. By the time it was made he was too sick to wear it, but he knew it was there in the kitchen. It may have made him think that someday he would be able to put it in.

Jean confessed that she hesitated at first to ask for volunteers from the community for fear of homophobia and revulsion against the disease, especially for fear that her young daughter in school might be affected. Nothing of this sort happened, or at least was ever expressed by anyone. The volunteers were faithful and efficient. All of them became very fond of the dying man.

Jude's tastes were fun to cater to. When I offered him a pear for dessert he asked shyly if he might have a bit of Stilton with it. In the refrigerator I could find only sliced and packaged Kraft cheese which he seemed to accept but, with his chef's delicacy still intact even if his teeth were not, he did not eat any of it.

My contribution to his entertainment was a few videos of Balanchine dances. He watched them once but did not want to see them again. Others brought tapes of classical music. But as he grew sicker and unable to leave his bed he lost interest in things beyond himself. His mind seemed to be on his body, the places where sores developed, his spinal abscess, the brittle tenderness in his bones. He stud-

Jude Bartlett. Photograph courtesy of Jean Hylan.

ied his feet which still bore the unmistakable calluses of a dancer.

"You have lovely feet," I said to him once while I rubbed his fleshless body with lotion.

He smiled, his charming boy's smile. "Yes, I do," he said.

Late in the afternoon on which he died, "just gave out," one of his caretakers said, some of us had gone to a meeting to be instructed in the changes in his care for what was expected to be his last days. Seated there and waiting, we were informed of his death. A great sadness, a deep silence settled over us. We stayed, seated around the table thinking about what we had done, and what Jude, the suffering, prematurely aged young man, had taught us about gentle mortality.

We spoke of our experiences with him. Most of the narrators were young, heterosexual couples, boat builders like Jean's husband, and a few single women and men of various sexual persuasions. One of them, a gay man who had often stayed the night with Jude, told us quietly that once, when Jude was restless, he asked if there was something he might do for him.

"Yes," he said. "You could come in bed with me and cuddle."

They lay together, "cuddling," for about an hour.

After this report there was silence. Then the wife of the boat builder who lives down the road from us in Sargentville said: "Yes. I know. Everybody needs to be cuddled sometimes."

It was a fine moment.

After the fever of Jude's life had cooled into death just before Thanksgiving last year, those of us who had known him had trouble adjusting to his absence from our schedules. Later, in the days and nights I was alone, he was back, not only in dreams but also present to me awake, his sweet voice asking for the herb tea he was too weak to drink and the exotic foods he remembered but could no longer eat.

Fran Lebowitz denied there was "such a thing as inner peace. There is only nervousness or death," she wrote. I thought not. Despite the outer turmoil created by the world (the nervousness), if one turns one's back on it there are moments of inner peace.

IF I have learned anything in these days, it is that the proper conditions for productive solitude are old age and the outside presence of a small portion of the beauty of the world. Given these, and the drive to explore and understand an inner territory, solitude can be an enlivening, even exhilarating experience. But when I was young, and eager to make my way in the world, I remember how painfully it turned into debilitating loneliness. For me, and for many others like me.

For the young: To be left alone with themselves when they are too unsure to respect the self they have been persuaded by the world's opinion to dislike, those who feel unworthy in the eyes of their families, what a terrible condition that is. The dismayingly high number of suicides among young persons attests to the consequences of such destructive isolation, that is, to their insurmountable loneliness.

Years ago, for a semester during the temporary absence of its director, I was left in charge of a writers' workshop at a university in the middle west. The heartland, as it was proudly termed by its poet-founder, was considered (by him) to be the perfect place to write. It was far from the fevered, distracting coasts, it gave the young writer space, time, and unlimited solitude in which to do good work.

I found the assignment trying, not so much the fiction workshop which was crammed with ambitious, productive, talented, often vain young writers, but the need to deal with their personal troubles and the problems they made me privy to. Being myself driven by an ineluctable desire to write at every possible moment, I resented their interruptions of my time and the psychic energy it required to tend to these demanding, creative souls. I had my own recalcitrant work to worry about.

One morning in my office, halfway through the semester, I listened to the complaints of a faculty member. One of his students, a man he said was "from Alaska, would you believe it?" (why he thought that should have strained my credibility more than his being from Grand Forks, North Dakota, or Moose Jaw, Saskatchewan, I was not sure) rarely attended the workshop and, on the few occasions he did, never said a word, "made no contribution," was the way he expressed it. He had never "put up," in the workshop jargon, any work for consideration and judgment by the others.

I said I would try to find out what was wrong with Eric Hunter (I will call him here). When he appeared in the office, I recognized him as the confused young man I had registered on the day before the semester began, the one who had not been able to find a place to live, indeed could not locate the office down the hall where such information was available. He was a strange-looking fellow, shorter than average, thin, and curiously pale for someone from the rugged north. His sandy hair was long and hung straight to his shoulders obscuring his ears and, if he bent forward, his pale eyes. His nose was oversized, very red, and hooked so that it seemed almost to touch his rosebud chin. Thus sadly endowed, he resembled no one so much as the buffoon in a Punch-and-Judy show.

In the interview he told me that, yes, he was not happy here; yes, it was true, he was working badly or not at all. He attributed his failure to his loneliness; he had made no friends. He laughed once, when I asked him if he might be homesick. "God, no," he said. Had he a girl he had left in Nome? I asked. No, neither there nor, for that matter, here. That was the trouble: he had never been able to capture the interest of women whose affection he desperately wanted. He said the women students here were too smart, too sophisticated, egotistical, and loftily scornful of him.

I could think of no words of comfort or advice except to urge him to work hard on his poems. Friends, I said, sometimes followed recognition of talent and accomplishment in this place, try for that. He said nothing except to thank me for my time. I never saw him again until, at three o'clock in the morning, halfway through the semester, someone in the emergency room of Mercy Hospital called to tell me Eric Hunter had been admitted to a ward there.

I went at once. When I was allowed to see him, he lay on his back, stretched out so flat that he looked like a cartoon character over which a steam roller had passed. He was unconscious, and his face was almost completely covered with bandages. Blood dripped into a vein in his arm; there was a tube in his mouth. I was told that he had driven himself to the hospital, had passed out from loss of blood in the parking lot, and was found by an intern leaving after his eighteen-hour stint. The nurse told me, with a shake of her head, that it appeared to the fellows in the emergency ward that Eric had been trying to cut off his face.

When his wounds had healed somewhat, and the danger of infection was passed, he was transferred to the mental ward of the hospital.

I called his parents in Nome. His father, mother, and two brothers came the next week. The three solidly built, bearded men in wool-flannel, plaid jackets and high leather boots had, to my eyes, no use for the poet Eric. His mother seemed always to be standing a little behind them when we talked and said nothing in defense of her son. She was small and bird-boned, much like Eric. Her skin was leathered and deeply wrinkled.

One brother, who laughed after every sentence he spoke, as if overcome with his own wit, described Eric's life at home. In the course of his description of Eric's failures and inadequacies he twice referred to him as a "faggot." His classmates in high school had nicknamed him " 'the purple flamingo,' so that gives you some idea of what we had to put up with," he said, and laughed. When I protested the faggot designation, telling his brother that Eric liked women and was troubled that they did not respond to him, his brother laughed and said: "Says who?"

I told Eric that his family wished to take him home with them. He was aghast. "I won't go. I want to stay and finish the year here." And then he added, rather pathetically, I thought: "It's all paid up." When I said that did not matter, he could reapply next summer and it would still be paid for, he said, almost as a plea of last resort: "I'm better. I promise, I won't do it again."

The doctor warned me that if he stayed I would be responsible for his welfare because, in his opinion, Eric was suicidal. It was then that I said the words, selfish, cowardly, and self-serving words for which, in recurring memory, I suffer profound guilt. I said I could not be responsible for him.

He went home. My assistant drove him and his family to the airport and reported to me that he had not said a word during the hour's ride.

The coda to this small saga of one short, beleaguered, and lonely life is this: Mrs. Hunter wrote to the poet-teacher of the workshop that, before the summer arrived in the north country, Eric Hunter shot himself in the head with one of his brother's guns. He died instantly and was buried in the Unitarian Church in Nome. After a private service, she had found some poems of Eric's with the name of his professor clipped to them. She enclosed them. One was titled "The Lonely Flamingo."

By this time I was settled back in the east, comfortable in my old study, safe in the wooden rocking chair I used for reading and note-taking, free (I thought) of all concern for anyone else. But of course I was not safe, would never be safe from the sight of his sad, unfortunate face. I will never be free of a sense of terrible inadequacy. I sent a lonely and desperate poet home alone to his cold country, in order to protect my warm self and my private concerns. Failing at first to deface himself, Eric Hunter ended his long loneliness by obliterating the rest of himself.

WHILE the world outside was dead with winter and ice, I kept alive on the kitchen table a small plant called oxalis. The leaves were blood red and wing-shaped or perhaps heart-shaped, even cloverlike, I couldn't tell which, and the flowers, five pale cups to a spindly stalk, grew directly from the soil, appearing to have no connection to the leaves.

But both shared one extraordinary trait. As darkness fell, they slowly folded in upon themselves. When it was entirely dark, they seemed to be one-dimensional, shy, retiring, private personages who had closed themselves off for the night.

In the morning, just as the first rays of the red sun appeared over the cove, I tried to observe them opening. But so gradual was the process of their unfolding I could never catch them at it. When the sky brightened, they were in full, opened session. I had missed the movement completely.

Since Tiny Alice, the name I gave the oxalis, was the only

flowering plant in the house, my attachment to her was strong. I took very good care of her. I decided that she operated exactly the way my mind does, shutting down without notice to hide its contents from me at the very moment of need, and then expanding, revealing something to me I had not expected.

❧ ODD: Yesterday, after an unexpected thaw, I felt myself literally growing larger, taller, even deeper when I looked out my study window at the wild world before me—the unplowed meadow full of frozen remnants, stumps, wild blackberry brambles, vestigial azalea bushes, granite stones, blackened fern stalks, dead weeds of every variety.

My small wilderness reminded me of places I had been, far from cities, where I was surrounded by untamed landscape. I thought of the edges of the Sangre de Cristo Mountains, so rough with undergrowth that the mountains seem to be rising up directly from one's tangled foot. I thought of the junglelike growths in Yucatan I had tried to plow through, each elevated place a mysterious, dense covering for broken stones that once may have been part of great temples. I remembered a deserted headland on Cape Breton where the fierce, uncontrollable sea assaulted the ancient rocks from every direction. . . .

Why did I feel this expansion of myself at the sight of wildness? I was not sure. But I did understand why crowded cities had the contrary effect on me. On those jammed streets, in high-rise offices and apartments, theaters, buses, restaurants, even museums (the throngs of people pushing at each other to get closer to Tutankhamen's gold-laden tomb, Matisse's great art), I felt shrunken, diminished. I closed down as Tiny Alice did when the shadows lengthened and the evening came.

Perhaps it was age. We shrink enough as we grow old. We do not need the hordes of civilization to intensify the process.

❧ ODD TOO: Submerged in the ideal climate for creating fiction, I found it absorbed me less than the remarks I was putting down about the climate itself. I borrowed an interesting book from the bookstore by Henri Nouwen called *Clowning in Rome* written fifteen years ago. He is reflecting on life as it is lived by members of religious communities, but what he says is true of life lived in the world. He observes that it is only in solitude, away from the persons with whom we ordinarily spend our time, that "we enter into a deeper intimacy with each other. It is a fallacy to think that we grow closer to each other when we talk, play, or work together. . . . In solitude our intimacy with each other is deepened."

I found this to be true. What others regard as retreat from them or rejection of them is not those things at all but instead a breeding ground for greater friendship, a culture for deeper involvement, eventually, with them. What I learned in solitude may make community with my friends and family possible, indeed fertile, whereas constant society was full of fruitless questions about their relation to me, my service to them, my value in the world.

In another book on the same subject (*Out of Solitude*) that I came upon later in the winter, Nouwen cites Mark's Gospel. The apostle reports that "in the morning, long before dawn, he [Jesus] got up and left the house and went off to a lonely place and prayed there." Nouwen reflects on the human need for such a "lonely place," without which "our lives are in danger."

Most meaningful to me were the effects he describes of a lack of solitude and silence in our fevered lives: "Somewhere we know that without silence *words lose their meaning* [these are my italics], that without listening speaking no longer heals, that without distance closeness cannot cure . . . without a lonely place our actions quickly become empty gestures."

❧ IN these harsh days of winter, when the distance between my cove and Deer Isle was one white, frozen stretch of land and water, I dressed in what up here we call "layers." I put on five pieces of clothing, beginning with underwear that covers the entire body and ending with wool sweaters and heavy, lined jeans. To go out I added another layer, a down jacket.

In this way, metaphorically, I now needed to live, with the top layer of my person known to the outside world and displayed for social purposes. But, close to the bone, there had to be an inner stratum, formed and cultivated in solitude, where the essence of what I was, am now, and will be, perhaps, to the end of my days, hides itself and waits to be found by the lasting silence.

114

❧ EARLY on the March morning when I left Sargentville for Washington to spend a month there and then further south in the sun, it was very cold, sixteen degrees below zero. The sea smoke on the water of the cove was stiff with frozen air, standing straight up in peaks and not moving, like tightly whipped cream.

I closed the door to the house which seemed to have a prescient, lonely air about it. I felt like a deserter who had heartlessly left behind someone who had sheltered her warmly against the harsh elements, against all the discouragement and disillusion of an inward journey.

"In every parting there is an image of death," observed George Eliot. Yes, I thought, but, like Dilsey in Faulkner's novel, I believed I would endure, even the death of the city. I would survive this parting and return here soon, to renew my acquaintance with myself. Like Don Quixote,
I have learned that, until death, it is all life.